A PASSION

FOR GOD

GREG LAURIE

HARVEST HOUSE PUBLISHERS
Eugene, Oregon 97402

Cover design by David Riley & Associates, Corona Del Mar, California

A PASSION FOR GOD
(Formerly titled *On Fire!*)
Copyright © 1998 by Greg Laurie
Published by Harvest House Publishers
Eugene, Oregon 97402

Library of Congress Cataloging-in-Publication Data

Laurie, Greg
    A passion for God / Greg Laurie.
        p.   cm.
    ISBN 1-56507-802-0
    1. Christian life.   I. Title.
BV4501.2.L3578   1998
248.4—dc21   97-40443
                                                             CIP

98 99 00 01 02 03 / BC / 10 9 8 7 6 5 4 3 2

To Chuck Smith
for his years of teaching
and living the principles found
in this book, and to L.E. Romaine
for helping a young kid learn
how to apply them.

Special thanks to
Carol Faulkner and Karen Daghar
for their help in preparation
of this book.

CONTENTS

PREFACE

I THINK YOU WOULD AGREE with me in observing that we are living in times that are full of great turmoil and uncertainty. All around us it seems like our society is literally coming apart at the seams. It seems like we have lost our moorings, our absolutes. It's as though we no longer have black and white, just varying shades of gray.

It appears this world of ours is going from bad to worse with no real end to this trend in sight. We live in times in which it seems that right is wrong and wrong is right.

This is not necessarily unique to our generation, for hundreds of years ago the prophet Isaiah decried the same perverse trend in his time when he said, "Woe to those who call evil good and good evil; who put darkness for light and light for darkness; who put bitter for sweet, and sweet for bitter!" (Isaiah 5:20).

If ever there was a moment when a far-sweeping spiritual awakening and revival is needed, the time is now.

The church of the first century dramatically impacted their world with the life-changing message of the gospel. It was said of them that they had turned their world upside down. I believe if we apply the same principles that they did and allow God's Holy Spirit to work through us the same can happen in our time.

What was their secret? In short, they had a burning passion for the Lord they served.

Jesus told us He would rather we be boiling hot or cold. If we are lukewarm He said He would spit us out of His mouth (Revelation 3:15,16).

What does it mean to have a passion for God?

That is what this book is about. We will follow the way that Jesus led and worked through a group of ordinary men and women who were filled with His power and did extra-ordinary things, touching their world with the life-changing message of the gospel.

We will see what the account of their lives, the book of Acts, has to say to us today. It is my prayer that as you read this book you will hear God's voice speak to you so that you will be able to say along with the two disciples who heard Jesus' words, "Did not our hearts burn within us while He talked with us on the road, and while He opened the Scriptures to us?" (Luke 24:32).

May God give to you a burning heart to make an impact on your world with the wonderful message of the gospel.

It may be later than we think.

𝒲HERE HAS THE PASSION GONE?

DO YOU REMEMBER THOSE first few days as a new believer? The excitement you felt. The indescribable joy you experienced. The burning desire you had to share it with others. In short, do you still feel that passion you first had for the Lord?

A letter I recently received from a listener to our radio program, A New Beginning, reminded me of that "first love" experience. See if you can relate to Adam's story:

> I was brought up in a non-religious family. The only time I ever went to church was when I spent the night at a friend's house and I'd have to go with them the next morning. Until about 6 months ago, I really had no idea what Christianity really was. I got a job driving blue-prints, and after awhile, the radio got really old. I began to listen to talk shows and, eventually, your show. My life has been forever changed since then.
>
> I have accepted Jesus Christ as my Lord and Savior, and I can't tell you the joy I have felt since then. My life has been changed forever in a matter of months! I'm reading the Bible every day, and my

9

love for the Lord grows deeper every day. . . . I really don't know the first thing about being a Christian. All I know is that Jesus is the most important thing to me right now. It's like nothing else matters in my life. I want to spend every minute reading the Bible and praying. Is this normal for someone who just discovered Jesus? I want the whole world to know what I'm feeling, but it's something I can't even describe on paper! I just had to tell someone how I felt and what Jesus has done for me.

I especially like Adam's question regarding his feelings and behavior: "Is it normal for someone who just discovered Jesus?" Yes, Adam, it is—and it *should* be the norm for every believer who has a burning passion to serve the Lord Jesus Christ. Tragically, however, many of us seem to have lost that passion. We are not making an impact on the morally bankrupt, spiritually destitute world around us. Instead, moral relativism and ungodly behavior seem to have found their way into our ranks as believers.

Turning the World Rightside Up

Can we return to that burning passion for God? Is it possible to really make a difference in our culture? Consider the believers of the first century church. On the day of Pentecost there were only 120 believers gathered in the upper room when the Holy Spirit was poured out. Their world was not too different from ours, and in some ways it was much worse. They lived under the jurisdiction of the godless Roman Empire. Immorality was rampant. The religious establishment was corrupt. Idolatry, spiritism, and demon worship were widely practiced. Everywhere the first Christians went they were ridiculed, opposed, and even persecuted for their beliefs. And yet within a period of 30 years, the original 120 and their converts came to be known as "these who have turned the world upside down" (Acts 17:6).

Despite any opposition, those early believers turned their world upside down—or more correctly, rightside up. They didn't allow the secular environment to turn them upside down or squeeze them into its mold. They made an impact for God on the immoral, ungodly world in which they were called to be witnesses of Jesus Christ.

How did the early church do it? In short, they had an undying passion for God.

John the Baptist introduced the ministry of Jesus by saying, "He who is coming after me is mightier than I. . . . He will baptize you with the Holy Spirit and fire" (Matthew 3:11). Moments before the resurrected Savior ascended into the clouds, He instructed His disciples, "Do not leave Jerusalem, but wait for the gift my Father promised, which you have heard me speak about. For John baptized with water, but in a few days you will be baptized with the Holy Spirit. . . . You will receive power when the Holy Spirit comes on you; and you will be my witnesses in Jerusalem, and in all Judea and Samaria, to the ends of the earth" (Acts 1:4,5,8, NIV).

Ten days later the promised fire fell when the Holy Spirit filled those 120 believers at Pentecost. The book of Acts records what can happen when a group of people with a fiery passion for God are turned loose in a needy world.

How do we get this fire back into our lives and our churches so we can influence our world like those early believers did? The answer: We need to rekindle the passion of our first love of the Lord. And we need the Holy Spirit's fire in our hearts so that our passion for God can blaze out through our lives and touch the world around us.

God's Cure for a Lost World

It's far too easy for believers to look at the world's problems and say, "Hey, I didn't have anything to do with this. Unbelievers and their rejection of God's standards are the source of all the immorality and ungodliness that is eating away at our society." But isn't it interesting that when God speaks of turning a nation around, He doesn't direct His comments to unbelievers? His Word gives *us* a clear blueprint for the job. Here it is: "If My people who are called by My name will humble themselves, and pray and seek My face, and turn from their wicked ways, then I will hear from heaven, and will forgive their sin, and heal their land" (2 Chronicles 7:14).

The cure, according to the Lord Himself, is *revival*. And it's not the world that needs reviving; the church does. Unbelievers are dead in sin. They need to come to faith in Christ. We who are Christians are already alive in Christ, but sometimes we're weak, anemic, lazy, asleep. We're the ones in need of revival. When we are revived, God will use us to bring unbelievers to life in Christ. When the church is turned rightside up through revival, the world will be turned rightside up.

When we follow God's blueprint for revival, the Lord will hear from heaven, forgive our sin, and heal our land. Psalm 84:11 says, "For the Lord God is a sun and shield; the Lord will give grace and glory; no good thing will He withhold from those who walk uprightly." Our responsibility is to attend to our walk with God, seeking daily to be what He has called us to be from the beginning. As we make obedience and faithfulness our focus, God promises to send healing both to our lives and our land.

What Can We Do?

This book is designed to help believers regain their original passion for God. There's no reason we can't turn the world rightside up as did those first-century Christians. But before I get to specifics, allow me to lay some groundwork by suggesting three key principles that underlie everything I'm about to say. If you fail to attend to these three guidelines, nothing in this book will benefit you in the least.

First, you need to revive the passion in your own heart. I'm not talking about seeking some cataclysmic, mountaintop emotional experience. I'm talking about returning to the basics of the dynamic Christian life as described in the book of Acts and the epistles. You will only revive the burning power and passion of Christ in your life by opening yourself to the power of God's Spirit, by anchoring your daily life in the disciplines of worship, Bible study, prayer, and faithful service, and by welcoming God's direction in the everyday routine of your life. These critical steps to personal revival are discussed in detail in Part One.

Second, you need to open your life to others so God's love within you can touch their lives as well. This means following God's guidelines for developing the oneness of biblical *koinonia* among the believers with whom you worship, study, pray, and work. Opening your life to others also means responding to God's command to reach out and disciple those around you who don't know Him. Sharing the passion in your heart with believers and unbelievers in your world is the theme of Part Two.

Third, you must be prepared to maintain the passion in your life when problems threaten to dampen and discourage your commitment to Christ. Some degree of persecution is a reality in the life of passionate believers. One promise we seldom hear believers "claim" but is certainly true is "all who desire to live godly in Christ Jesus will suffer persecution" (2 Timothy 3:12). In addition, other trials and temptations will afflict us. Remember Paul's words in Acts 14:22: "Through many hardships we must enter the kingdom of God." Part Three will equip you to find the courage and perseverance you need to endure those times of disillusionment and disappointment so you can continue to live out your priorities as a child of God in an ungodly world.

Revival Begins with You

I wish most Christians would serve the Lord with the same intensity that they used to have when they served the devil. Can you imagine what a difference that would make in our lives? That is the type of passionate faith that the Lord desires. He wants us to completely dedicate our lives to Him, leaving no room for compromise. He longs to hear us say, "I am not going to compromise in my business. I am not going to compromise with my wife or husband. I am not going to compromise with my kids. I am not going to compromise in any area. I am going to live a sold-out life for Jesus Christ." That, my friend, is the first step to reviving your passion for God.

The most miserable person is the person who tries to live in two worlds. It just doesn't work. In the end, you get nothing. It's a complete break.

When revival breaks out in the lives of individual Christians, God's people begin to function as they ought to. And when we begin functioning as we should, all the problems of our society can be addressed. Prejudice, crime, the breakdown of the family, immorality, drugs—all of them can be affected in the wake of a far-reaching national spiritual revival.

Did you know that every great social movement in America was birthed in revival? The nineteenth-century revivals of Charles and John Wesley, for example, had a dramatic, positive impact on such problems as slavery, inhumane treatment in prisons, liquor traffic, and poor education. Moral reform has never brought about spiritual revival, but spiritual revival always brings about moral reform.

You can work until you are blue in the face trying to patch up this crumbling world of ours. Or you can get to the root of the problem by praying first for your heart and then for Christ's church.

Where is your passion today? We can do all of the right things outwardly—attend church, read the Bible, say the right things—but still have a deadened heart. Our passion for God can easily slip into a passion for the fading things of this life.

Ask yourself these questions: Are you living your life in a way that is upward, inward, and outward? Do you long to spend time with your Savior? Are you seeking to glorify God with your abilities that God has given to you? Do you endeavor to build up others with the gifts that the Lord has instilled in your life? Are you seeking to get the gospel out in your sphere of influence? If you sense that your passion needs to be stirred again, you might pray along with the psalmist, "Will you not revive us again, that Your people may rejoice in You?" (Psalm 85:6). May this prayer reignite your passion for God as you read the pages ahead.

PART ONE

BUILDING THE PASSION

$\mathcal{P}$OWER BEYOND OURSELVES

A TOWN SOMEWHERE in the U.S. was battered one night by hurricane-force winds. In the morning, after the storm had abated, the citizens emerged from their homes and shelters to assess the damage. The power of the storm quickly became clear to one investigator who was dumbfounded by an incredible discovery. Mouths dropped open as people came to check out his report: a common plastic drinking straw driven deep into a telephone pole by the night's vicious winds. Obviously, under normal circumstances, a flimsy straw could never penetrate a telephone pole. But the tremendous power of the wind had driven the straw into the wood like a spike.

As believers living in an ungodly world, sometimes we wonder if we can ever make a difference. We wonder if we can effectively penetrate our cynical culture with the good news God has given us to proclaim. The answer lies in the source of our power. If we rely on our own strength and methods, then no, we cannot make much of a difference. But if we choose to be driven by God's limitless power, we become like that straw in the hurricane where nothing can stop us. We can indeed make a dramatic difference.

Waiting for Power

Where did the early Christians find the power to turn their world rightside up for God? The first group had to wait for it. Shortly before His ascension, Jesus told His disciples, "Do not leave Jerusalem, but wait for the gift my Father promised, which you have heard me speak about" (Acts 1:4, NIV). At this point, it was clear that the disciples were not yet fully equipped for the task of world evangelism. Peter had encountered some rough times in recent weeks. The night before Jesus' crucifixion he denied his Lord three times. If Peter could be demoralized so easily, how could he be expected to stand before thousands and testify of Jesus? Peter and the other disciples needed power beyond themselves. For that reason Jesus told them to wait in Jerusalem until the power He promised them arrived.

Furthermore, the disciples didn't yet understand what Jesus was doing. They asked Him, "Lord, will You at this time restore the kingdom to Israel?" (Acts 1:6). They still thought Jesus was going to establish an earthly kingdom to overthrow the Romans. This was the hope they nurtured all along. When He was crucified, their expectation for a messianic kingdom on earth was dashed. But with His resurrection, their hopes were revived. So they pressed Him on the issue again.

Jesus didn't answer their question directly, but instead replied, "It is not for you to know times or seasons which the Father has put in His own authority. But you shall receive power when the Holy Spirit has come upon you; and you shall be witnesses to Me" (vv. 7,8). In essence, He told them, "Don't be concerned about when My earthly kingdom will be established, but rather focus your attention on what you should be doing while you await it. That's why you must wait in Jerusalem until you are empowered by the Holy Spirit."

Most of us would probably love to know when Jesus is coming back—but God is not going to give us an exact time or date. His answer to us is the same one He gave to His disciples 2000 years ago: Focus your attention on the task at hand, not the trip ahead. We have opportunities today that may not remain available and open doors that may soon close. We can't allow ourselves to become so preoccupied with the future that we overlook the present. We need to take hold of the unique opportunities God sets before us each day.

But to do so, we need power beyond ourselves. And that's just what Jesus promised us: "You shall receive power when the Holy Spirit has come upon you." The ineffectiveness of the church today is largely due to our neglect of the power that set the first-century church into motion. Programs have taken the place of power. Gimmicks have taken the place of the gospel. Many years ago, A.W. Tozer said that if the Holy Spirit were taken away from the New Testament church, 90 percent of what they did would come to a halt. But if the Holy Spirit were taken away from today's church, only 10 percent of what it does would cease. We're not seeing the same results as the early believers because we're not relying on the same power they did.

Yet God can still work in the lives of Christians today as He worked in the first century. Consider the nation of China. Beginning in the nineteenth century, Western missionaries ministered to the people of that country for 100 years and reaped about 800,000 converts. Then the communist revolution took place and Mao Tse-tung threw out the Westerners. Chinese Christians lost their churches and Bibles. Many believers were tortured and even put to death for their faith. Western Christians wondered whether the church in China would survive the intense persecution.

So how did these believers fare under 40 years of communist rule with almost none of the resources we consider essential? When Western Christians were readmitted into the country and allowed to see how the Chinese church had managed during those turbulent years, they were astonished. The church had not floundered; it had flourished, increasing by as many as 75 million converts!

How did they do it? They got back to the basics, took God at His Word, and laid hold of the same power the early church employed. Vance Havner once said, "We are not going to move this world by criticism of it nor conformity to it, but by the combustion within it of lives ignited by the Spirit of God." The Chinese church, thriving and advancing even under communism, is living proof of his words. This power is still available to the church.

Power to Perform

The word for power Jesus uses in Acts 1:8 is the Greek word *dunamis*, from which we get the words dynamite, dynamic, and dynamo. While the word obviously had not yet taken on those meanings when Jesus used it, nevertheless it's clear He was describing something dynamic and potent, something that can turn ordinary Christians into extraordinary Christians.

Because of the nature of *dunamis*, it is important to understand the role of emotions in the outworking of God's power in our lives. Since it is possible to have an emotional response to what God does in us, we must distinguish between emotion and emotionalism. Emotion can be a very good thing. We can feel joy, excitement, or happiness when God answers our prayers or uses us in a special way. The problem comes when we enter the realm of emotionalism, attempting to live constantly on the plane of good feelings.

Let's suppose you're in a worship service and feel God's powerful presence in a special way. That's wonderful! But if you expect every worship service to replicate that feeling, you have passed from emotion to emotionalism. Sadly, some believers don't believe they are relating to God unless they have a dramatic feeling of His presence. And when they don't feel God's presence, they can't seem to relate to Him.

Or imagine that you are sharing your faith with a non-Christian neighbor and you're exhilarated by the sensation of God's power operating in your life at that moment. Great! But if in the future you judge whether God is using you by the presence or absence of that sense of exhilaration, you're into emotionalism. God didn't pour out the power of the Holy Spirit to make us *feel* something but to help us *accomplish* something. God's power is practical power. Enjoy the good feelings when they happen, but don't let the lack of feelings prevent you from stepping out in the power of the Spirit to do what God wants you to do.

It's like the difference between dynamite and a dynamo. A stick of dynamite explodes and makes a big impact in only seconds, then it's all over. A dynamo, a machine designed to generate power so work can be accomplished, just keeps running. Sometimes God's power is like dynamite in our lives, blasting us emotionally, jolting us out of our complacency, motivating us to some great step of growth or feat of ministry. We see a lot of these explosions in the miracles and wonders that highlight the book of Acts.

But in between these explosive moments, God's power is like a strong, steady-running motor inside us that helps us live from day to day at a level we can't achieve in our own strength. This is the power that keeps us operating between emotional highs and mountaintop experiences. Never underestimate the importance of God's explosive "dynamite power" in your life. But by the same token, be aware that God's dynamic "dynamo power" is available every moment and every day to help you be what God wants you to be and accomplish what He wants you to accomplish.

As the saying goes, it's not how high you jump that counts, it's how straight you walk when you hit the ground. I don't care how loudly you shout hallelujah, how long you sing, or how great you feel emotionally or spiritually. If your dynamite experiences aren't matched by a practical, daily dynamo lifestyle, your emotional highs don't mean much. God's power is practical and especially designed to affect our daily walk inside and outside the church.

We get a better picture of the kind of power Jesus is talking about when we see how *dunamis* and its verb form *dunamai* are used elsewhere in the New Testament. It should encourage you to know that the power Jesus promises us is the same kind of power God exerted to raise Christ from the dead and seat Him in heaven (Ephesians 1:19,20). This same supernatural power is present in you by God's Spirit to:

- cause you to overflow with hope (Romans 15:13);
- help you bear up under and escape temptation (1 Corinthians 10:13);
- equip you to be a servant of God (Ephesians 3:7);
- give you inner strength (Ephesians 3:16);
- allow God to do more than you can ask or imagine in and through your life (Ephesians 3:20);
- equip you to resist Satan (Ephesians 6:11);
- provide endurance and patience (Colossians 1:11);
- help you work hard for Him (Colossians 1:29);

- shield you (1 Peter 1:5);
- provide everything you need for life and godliness (2 Peter 1:3).

No wonder the early church had such a dramatic impact upon their world. They were power-packed! It's wonderful to know that the very same power that raised Jesus from the dead, gave Peter boldness, saved unbelievers, caused miracles, and much more is just as available to us today!

Power for a Purpose

In Acts 1:8, Jesus tells us the ultimate purpose of God's power in our lives: to be His witnesses. The word "witness" comes from the Greek word *martus*, which is where we get our English word "martyr." This doesn't mean that every empowered witness will become a martyr. But in light of the suffering and death of many Christians over the centuries, Jesus seems to be saying, "You shall receive dynamic power to *live* for Me and, if necessary, even to *die* for Me."

The word "witness" is used 29 times in the book of Acts as either a verb or a noun. A witness is someone who tells others what he has seen and heard. The apostles had this understanding when they said in Acts 4:20, "We cannot but speak the things which we have seen and heard."

If you were a witness in a court of law and were called to testify, the judge and jury wouldn't be interested in your personal opinion about the guilt or innocence of the person on trial. What they want from you are the facts about what you observed. You might say, "I think the defendant is guilty. Just look at him! He has shifty eyes. He just looks guilty!" But the court isn't interested in your opinion. It only wants you to describe what you saw and heard.

Likewise, we as Christ's witnesses are empowered to proclaim what we have seen and heard about our Savior. Witnessing means telling others what Christ has done for us and what He has shown us in His Word. Our daily witness includes our Spirit-empowered words as well as our Spirit-empowered walk. I frequently hear Christians say, "Let's go witness and share our faith," and that's great. But in reality, a witness is as much what we are as what we say and do. Without God's power in our lives we are ill-equipped to be the witnesses He called us to be.

Where are we to be His witnesses? We know that Jesus wants His people to reach out to the whole world with the gospel. He gave us our marching orders after His resurrection and before His ascension: "Go into all the world and preach the gospel to every creature" (Mark 16:15).

"But reaching the world is such an enormous task!" you say. "Where do I start?" This reminds me of the question, "How do you eat an elephant?" The answer is, "One bite at a time!" The same is true of the work of world evangelism. It takes place "one bite at a time."

In Acts 1:8 we have God's strategy for world evangelism "bite by bite" or step by step: "You shall be witnesses to Me in Jerusalem, and in all Judea and Samaria, and to the end of the earth." Pay special attention to the significance of the order.

The first stop was to be Jerusalem. Jerusalem was home base for the church, representing her own backyard. Your Jerusalem is the neighborhood and town where you live.

The second stop was Judea. This area was located all around Jerusalem, representing the disciples' larger community. Your Judea may encompass the county or state where your town is located.

The third stop was Samaria. This province north of Judea was home to a racially mixed segment of people that the Jews despised. It was definitely "the other side of the tracks." Your Samaria may be anyplace nearby where people of a different race, culture, or socioeconomic level live.

The fourth stop was the end of the earth. Many of Jesus' disciples left familiar surroundings and traveled great distances as His witnesses. This represents global outreach far beyond our borders.

Sometimes the life of a person on the foreign mission field sounds so glamorous and exciting. You hear veteran missionaries tell of their great travels for Christ and all the people they led to faith. So you begin to daydream, *I sure would like to be a missionary. I want to travel somewhere far away and just tell people about the Lord. That would be so wonderful.*

No matter how sincere your intentions may be, you must start with home base. You don't need to cross the sea to be a witness; you can start by crossing the street! Your mission field is all around you. If you are not willing to be a witness where you live, don't expect God to give you opportunities elsewhere. Be faithful where you are and He may open even greater opportunities for you in other places.

The Dynamic Difference

Ten days after Jesus ascended into heaven, the Holy Spirit descended upon the obediently waiting 120 disciples in the upper room (Acts 2:1-4). What difference did the empowering of the Holy Spirit make in the lives of these early believers? The same disciples who huddled behind closed doors after Jesus' crucifixion for fear of the Jews could not be kept behind closed doors after they had received this "heavenly dynamite." After God's power exploded in their lives, they had the courage to tell the authorities, "We cannot but speak the things which we have seen and heard" (Acts 4:20). And Peter, who had denied Jesus publicly two months earlier, immediately began preaching to a huge crowd in Jerusalem and welcomed 3000 converts. The disciples were transformed into people of power. They were on fire.

God's power still makes a difference in people's lives today. What about you? Do you desire greater boldness in your witness for Christ? Has your prayer life become dry and one-dimensional? Do you fail to see any gifts of the Spirit at work in your life? Do you feel that you're lacking something in your spiritual walk? Is the world turning you upside down instead of you turning your world rightside up?

If you've answered yes to these questions, then you are a perfect candidate for the power of God's Spirit to transform your life. What could be hindering your experience of God's power? Perhaps it's unbelief. Unbelief is probably the greatest obstacle to the Spirit's work. Matthew 13:58 records that when Jesus returned to His hometown, "He did not do many mighty works there because of their unbelief." Interestingly, the phrase "mighty works" in this verse is once again the Greek word *dunamis*. Jesus could not display His full power because of the unbelief of the people.

Unbelief is the barrier you erect when you say, "I don't think God can work powerfully in my life." And when you don't believe God can exercise His power through you, that's just what happens. It's your own fault if you are not receiving anything from the Lord or doing anything for the Lord. It's no different than placing your hand over your cup and saying "No, thank you" when the waitress comes around with more coffee. Through unbelief you've placed your hand over your life and told God that you're not interested in what He can say to you and do through you.

The promise of God's power is as valid for you as it was for the church in the book of Acts. Peter said during his first sermon, "The promise is to you and to your children, and to all who are afar off, as many as the Lord our God will call" (Acts 2:39). Are you called? If you're a Christian, of course you are! God's promise of power is for you. The first step to realizing and employing God's power to have an impact on your world is to say, "Lord, I believe Your power is for me. I believe You want to do dynamic things in me and through me by the power of Your Spirit. So fill me, Lord, with Your dynamic power that I might turn my world rightside up for Jesus Christ."

"Okay," you say, "I believe God can empower me with His Holy Spirit. Now what do I do?"

Dunamis is not an impersonal force. *Dunamis* is God's Holy Spirit exercising His power in our lives. People of power are people of the Spirit. If you want God's power flooding your life, you need God's Spirit flooding your life.

Sadly, over the centuries the Scriptures concerning the Holy Spirit and His power have been misinterpreted and twisted. Today there is tremendous confusion regarding the Spirit-filled life. It is vital that we understand what the Bible means when it speaks of the Spirit-filled life so that we don't miss the genuine for the counterfeit. That's what we'll take a look at next.

CHAPTER TWO

EMBRACING THE GENUINE, REJECTING THE COUNTERFEIT

PEOPLE WITH A PASSION FOR GOD, who are turning their world rightside up for Christ, are people filled and empowered by the Holy Spirit. That's why the infant church made such an impact on its world. On the day of Pentecost, the Holy Spirit was poured out on the church in Jerusalem in dramatic, never-to-be-repeated fashion (Acts 2:1-4). The power that energized the early Christians flowed out of the Holy Spirit's infilling. The Acts of the Apostles, as this book is titled, could just as easily be called the Acts of the Holy Spirit through the Apostles.

Before Pentecost, godly people were only periodically filled with the Holy Spirit. The Spirit came upon certain people at certain times for certain tasks, then He left them. As an example, in the Old Testament we find the Holy Spirit coming upon Elijah to work a miracle and upon Samson to accomplish a great physical feat and upon David as he worshiped the Lord on his stringed instrument. The Holy Spirit did not dwell in these people from day to day. But from Pentecost on, He took up permanent residence in the lives of all who come to God through faith in Christ. If you're a Christian, the Holy Spirit lives within you (Romans 8:9). And the same power that energized the first-century believers to dramatically impact their world is available today to all who are indwelt by the Holy Spirit.

Sadly, the Holy Spirit's role in the life of the believer has been horribly misrepresented in recent times. Some Christians believe that you must have a great emotional experience with God in order to be genuinely empowered by the Holy Spirit. Others believe that you become a kind of spiritual oddball when you invite the Holy Spirit into your life. Neither is true.

God's Spirit moves powerfully yet *practically*. Paul wrote, "God has not given us a spirit of fear, but of power and of love and of a sound mind" (2 Timothy 1:7). The phrase "of a sound mind" describes a well-balanced, disciplined mind. You don't need to check your brain at the door to be a Spirit-led, Spirit-empowered Christian.

When we see bizarre antics performed in the name of the Holy Spirit, our tendency is to recoil and say, "If that's what it means to live in the power of the Spirit, I don't want anything to do with it." But just because some have misused and twisted the Scriptures, don't conclude that God's Spirit doesn't want to do a genuine, powerful, sound-minded work in the lives of believers today. He does. The key is understanding and following what God's Word says about the ministry of the Holy Spirit.

Finding a Happy Medium

Believers often fall into one of two camps regarding the ministry and gifts of the Holy Spirit. One extreme emphasizes the work of the Holy Spirit in practically everything they say and do. They have conferences on the Spirit, sing songs about the Spirit, and constantly talk about the work and the gifts of the Spirit. Often they are so busy seeking direct revelations from the Spirit of God that they over-look the clear written revelation in the Word of God. Although these believers may have a genuine love for the Lord, their desire to witness "power" has led them into unscriptural practices.

At the other end of the spectrum we have Christians whose focus is on Bible exposition. They study the Word, learn the Word, and memorize the Word (as we all should). Unfortunately, however, sometimes these zealous students of Scripture are close-minded to the working of God's Spirit. They can be very knowledgeable about the Spirit and yet quench the Spirit by not allowing Him to move in their lives outside their time-honored traditions.

The key is balance: knowing the Word of God and implementing the practical power of God's Spirit. God's Word gives us absolutes, guarding us from ill-conceived teachings and self-proclaimed prophets with a false mes-sage. Like the Bereans, we should examine every teaching and experience by the Scriptures "to find out whether these things [are] so" (Acts 17:11). This is precisely how the Spirit of God works through the Word of God.

I can't think of a better example of balance between God's Word and God's Spirit than Calvary Chapel in Costa Mesa, California. Chuck Smith, the pastor, began this min-istry with 25 people in a home Bible study. After 25 years they have a regular attendance (not names on the church roll, but people actually attending) of some 20,000! Not only that, but there are over 800 Calvary Chapel affili-ates—many of which have congregations numbering 5000 or more.

What explains the phenomenal success of Calvary Chapel and its branch ministries around the world? Chuck Smith's answer is disarmingly simple: "It is the Spirit of

God working through the Word of God in the hearts of the people of God."

The apostle Peter understood this balance. On the day of Pentecost, he was able to explain from Scripture the incredible experience that caused some to think the disciples were drunk. He said, "This is what was spoken by the prophet Joel" (Acts 2:16). Peter declared the experience valid because it was based in God's Word.

Peter had many wonderful spiritual experiences with Jesus before Pentecost, including the transfiguration when the Lord's majesty was revealed. Later, when writing about this experience, Peter said, "We also have the prophetic word made more sure, which you do well to heed as a light that shines in a dark place" (2 Peter 1:19). In essence he was saying, "Yes, I have seen many of these things with my own eyes, but I don't base my belief in Jesus on my personal experiences alone. I base my faith on the 'prophetic word,' the Word of God."

Anyone who claims a spiritual experience and yet can't say, "This is what is spoken in the Word of God," should stop deceiving himself. Any so-called spiritual phenomenon or experience that isn't founded solidly on Scripture should be abandoned.

A Profile of the Holy Spirit

People have many misconceptions regarding the work and ministry of the Holy Spirit, undoubtedly because of the many bizarre and unusual exhibitions said to be inspired by Him. Consequently, many Christians recoil from anything that smacks of the Holy Spirit, fearing that they too will end up exhibiting the same bizarre behavior.

This, of course, is unfortunate. The Holy Spirit is greatly grieved by many of the antics being blamed on Him these days. He has a distinct and important work in this world, as well as in the life of the believer, and it is a great tragedy to miss out on that work because of misrepresentation and ignorance.

If our spiritual experiences are to line up with the Word of God, it is vital that we have a basic understanding of who the Holy Spirit is. Some wrongly assume that the Spirit is more of an *it* than a *Him*. This may be due in part to a misunderstanding of the portrait we have of Him in Scripture, where He is described as being like the wind or being in the form of a dove, and so forth. Yet we must balance these images with those we find for the rest of the Trinity.

After all, Jesus referred to Himself as the bread of life, the door, and the vine. Do these images really mean that Jesus is a loaf of bread or an actual door? Of course not! Likewise, God the Father is referred to as a refuge and a consuming fire. Does this mean that He is literally a rock fortress or a blasting furnace? Of course not! These are merely symbols to help our finite minds grasp certain attributes of the Godhead—Father, Son, and Holy Spirit.

Neither is the Holy Spirit an impersonal force or power. When speaking of this member of the Trinity, Jesus said, "When He, the Spirit of truth, has come, He will guide you into all truth. He will glorify Me" (John 16:13,14).

Jesus identified the Holy Spirit as a person, a *He*. Furthermore, personal actions are attributed to the Holy Spirit throughout Scripture. For instance, the Spirit speaks (Acts 13:2), teaches (John 14:26), intercedes (Romans 8:26), gives commands (Acts 13:2), and ordains (Acts 20:28). In addition, as a person, the Holy Spirit can be offended. The New Testament specifically mentions six sins which can be committed against the Holy Spirit. It's only possible to "sin against" a person; you can't sin against an impersonal force or an inanimate object.

It's great to know that we believers are not influenced by a "force" but by a Person, a Person who is very God Himself and whose purpose is to conform us to the image of Christ.

The Spirit-Controlled Life

The Spirit-filled, Spirit-empowered life is well-illustrated in the story of Stephen in the book of Acts. Stephen was "a man full of . . . the Holy Spirit" (Acts 6:5). The word "full" in this verse can also be translated "controlled by." How did Stephen exemplify the Spirit-controlled life? He was full of faith and wisdom, he served widows, preached the gospel boldly, and was martyred for standing up to the unrighteous Jewish leaders. Yet his boldness and death made a major impact on one of those leaders who later became the most influential disciple of the first century: the apostle Paul. Stephen was on fire in the Spirit, and though he didn't live to see it, he changed his world for God.

Ephesians 5:18 exhorts us, "Be filled with the Spirit." Literally translated, this phrase says, "Be constantly filled with the Spirit." In other words, being filled with the Spirit is not just a one-time event; it's absolutely necessary to come back for refills again and again! It's a constant, ongoing process of welcoming the presence and power of the Holy Spirit into your life.

Moreover, the original Greek renders this phrase in the imperative. God is not merely suggesting you be filled with the Spirit; He is commanding you to be constantly refilled. He wants you to take hold of all the resources He has made available to you.

Note that Stephen's Spirit-controlled life didn't send him to some euphoric state. Acts does specify, however, that he was under the control of the Spirit of God and became a powerful witness for Christ. That's exactly what Jesus said would happen when the Holy Spirit came (Acts 1:8)—and Stephen experienced the full definition of the word "witness" (*martus*) by giving his life.

Because the Holy Spirit controlled every aspect of Stephen's life, he had the ability to stand up before his accusers and testify to what he believed. You may be thinking, *I can never do what Stephen did.* Yes, you can! Not in your own abilities or strengths, but in the power of the Spirit. What was available to Stephen is also available to you. Remember Paul's words to the believers in Philippi: "I can do all things through Christ who strengthens me" (Philippians 4:13).

The Proof of the Pudding Is in the Eating

We all know that many of the activities attributed to the Holy Spirit have little, if anything, to do with Him. It's been said, "The proof of the pudding is in the eating," or to put it biblically, "By their fruit you will recognize them" (Matthew 7:16, NIV). What is the evidence of infilled believers? Practical results. In the book of Galatians, Paul tells us the natural outgrowth of being filled with the Holy Spirit is "love, joy, peace, longsuffering, kindness, goodness, faithfulness, gentleness, self-control" (5:22,23).

Spirit-filled believers will enjoy great feelings and the use of spiritual gifts. The fruit of joy and peace can't be beat! However, the Spirit-filled life also shows itself practically in longsuffering and self-control. Walking in the Spirit should be seen in the worship service and in the workplace. It should be evident in the church and in the home.

What does it mean to be filled by the Spirit? Three word pictures in the Greek help us understand what the term "filled" means.

First, it was used of the wind filling a sail and pushing a boat through the water. To be filled with the Spirit is to be moved along by God Himself. He becomes our source of motivation. When we are filled with the Spirit, following His commands becomes a delight instead of a drudgery. That's why the apostle John could write, "This is love for God: to obey his commands. And his commands are not burdensome" (1 John 5:3, NIV).

Second, being filled carries the idea of permeation and was used of salt permeating meat in order to flavor it and preserve it. God wants His Spirit to permeate our lives and influence everything we think, say, and do.

Third, being filled means to be under the control of something or someone. A person who is filled with sorrow is no longer in complete control of himself but is controlled by that emotion. He can't stop weeping. He can't concentrate on his responsibilities. A person filled with anger, fear, jealousy, etc., is also under the control of that overpowering emotion.

Being filled with the Spirit is similar, only in a much more positive sense. It means placing every thought, every decision, every act under the Spirit's control. Galatians 5:16 promises, "Walk by the Spirit, and you will not carry out the desire of the flesh" (NASB). When you walk in the Spirit you have the resources to do what God wants you to do and not do what God doesn't want you to do.

Are you controlled by the Spirit right now? You must be if you are to be the man or woman God uses to turn your world rightside up. Go to Him right now in prayer and ask Him to refill you and give you a heartfelt passion for God.

CHAPTER THREE

TAKE TIME TO GET WELL GROUNDED

WE'RE USED TO GETTING information fast and bite-sized. We can't wait for the 11 P.M. news; we want to know what's going on *right now*. Turn on CNN any hour of the day and in just minutes you can find out what's happening globally. Better yet, in many cases you can watch history live as it happens, as much of the world did during the Tiananmen Square massacre and the Persian Gulf war. These days, candidates campaigning for office must distill their vision into 10-second "sound bites." Few people will sit still long enough to listen to a 30-minute speech.

We are a nation on the go. We are no longer confined to the office; we can take our work home with us through the technology of notebook computers and fax machines. We don't have to waste time eating in a sit-down restaurant; we can drive through a fast-food place and eat on the go. And, thanks to cellular phone technology, we can now drive, eat, and talk on the phone all at the same time (just be careful not to mistake your receiver for your burrito!). Recently I saw a man in the airport with a cellular phone up to each ear, very loudly carrying on two conversations at once!

As we have become accustomed to this frantic pace of life, we sometimes expect God to adapt Himself to our busy schedules. We know that daily Bible study is important. But with our days so tightly packed, we scour the Christian bookstore for titles promising a complete daily devotional in only a few moments so we can fit our Bible reading into our busy schedule. We also know prayer is vital to our spiritual health. But we get so busy that we end up with only a few minutes at bedtime to talk to God, and we're usually asleep before we say amen. We understand the importance of worship and fellowship with other believers. But with all our other activities, we believe we're doing well just to get to one or two services a week—and forget about volunteering to help out at the church.

If you want to develop a passion for God so He can use you to have an impact on your world for Him, it's time to slow down and evaluate your priorities. Consider Jesus' words to Martha. Perhaps you remember the story from Luke 10:38-42. One day Jesus came to visit His good friends, sisters Mary and Martha, for a meal. As He sat down to impart some spiritual truths, Mary quickly seized the moment and sat down at His feet to drink in His every word.

Martha, no doubt out of love, went into the kitchen to prepare the feast. But when she realized she would be doing all the work without her sister's help, she became frustrated and burst in on Jesus and Mary, demanding some assistance. In response, Jesus gently said, "Martha, Martha, you are worried and troubled about many things. But one thing is needed, and Mary has chosen that good part, which will not be taken away from her" (10:41,42). Martha wasn't doing anything wrong, but her busyness was keeping her from a higher priority: time spent with Jesus.

Have you ever felt like a modern-day Martha, so caught up in the activities of daily life that you find your spiritual life flickering instead of blazing? Like Martha, you need to learn from Mary's example to slow down and value sitting at Jesus' feet. Your relationship with Jesus cannot consist of five-minute devotionals or 10-second "prayer bites." Instead of expecting God to adapt to your hectic schedule, you must adapt to His.

That's one of the primary reasons why the early Christians were ablaze for God. Acts 2:42 summarizes it concisely: "They continued steadfastly in the apostles' doctrine and fellowship, in the breaking of bread, and in prayers." In the midst of all the activity around them, these fired-up believers set aside specific time to learn, to fellowship and worship with each other, and to pray. Their persistent attention to these critical disciplines paved the way for the mighty works God accomplished through them.

In this chapter we will look more closely at the priority of learning at Jesus' feet. In Chapter 4 we'll consider briefly the complementary disciplines of congregational worship and fellowship. And in Chapter 5 we will examine the vital role of prayer in the life of a passionate Christian.*

A Thriving Believer Is a Learning Believer

Those early Christians devoted themselves to the apostles' teaching, which has come down to us in the form of the Bible. God's Word is essential for any believer who wants to flourish spiritually. You must be regularly and consistently committed to the study of the Word of God if you hope to maintain your passion for God and help turn your

---

* I must give credit to John Stott for his excellent outline of Acts 2 from his commentary on the book of Acts, *The Spirit, the Church and the World* (Downers Grove, IL: InterVarsity Press).

world rightside up. If you suffer a breakdown at this level, everything else we discuss in this book is irrelevant. Show me a Christian who is lax in his reading and study of the Scripture, and I will show you a Christian who is floundering in all aspects of his life.

What about you? Have you looked into the Scripture today? It's been said, "Seven days without reading the Bible will make one weak." If you feel spiritually anemic and powerless, chances are you're trying to scrimp by on less than your "minimum daily requirement" of God's Word.

Some who claim to be more interested in spiritual phenomena might say, "I'm not into doctrine, I just want to love Jesus." But if you really want to know Jesus and grow in your love for Him, you must study doctrine. If you don't believe in something, you're liable to fall for anything! In other words, if your heart and mind are not securely anchored in God's Word, you can easily drift off into one of the many false teachings that are plaguing the church today. It is important to realize that success or failure in the Christian life is dependent on how much of the Word of God we get into our heart and life on a regular basis and how obedient we are to it.

Acts 2:42 mentions that the early believers "continued steadfastly" in the apostles' doctrine and the other disciplines. This is a crucial point, for it speaks of a real passion these Christians shared for the Word of God. They did not have a casual attitude toward Bible study or any aspect of their life together. They were firm, fixed, settled, and established in their commitment to learn God's Word.

By contrast, a lot of Christians today approach involvement in God's Word like some dieters approach the "battle of the bulge." You know you should shed several pounds, so you sign up for membership at the local health club. You're fired up at the prospect of returning to form.

Initially, the novelty of the high-tech exercise machines and the excitement of getting back into shape motivate you to give it your all. But after a few days your fervor starts to fizzle. Your muscles ache and your belly doesn't seem to be shrinking. You doggedly decide to hang in there, but soon schedules conflict and eventually you lose even the will to try. You then become a member in name only. You've lost your passion.

Sadly, people often go through this type of experience in their Bible study. They start out with a bang but end with a whimper. At first the excitement of new truths electrifies and challenges them. But as time goes on, the novelty wears off. The day-to-day commitment of being a real disciple of Jesus Christ annoys them, and many lose interest. They lose their passion for God's Word.

Some think it was easy for first-century believers to continue steadfastly in the Word because they were living in a "first love" relationship with Jesus Christ. Like a newlywed couple still in the honeymoon phase, those first Christians pursued their spiritual goals with enthusiasm. But what happened when the initial glow of their "first love" wore off? Were they still as committed to learning God's Word?

Remember: The book of Acts covers a period of about 30 years. Yet we see Christians from Chapter 1 through Chapter 28 ardently studying the Scriptures and eagerly applying them to their lives. Their commitment to God's Word remained steadfast long after the first excitement drained away.

You may not *feel* as excited about being a Christian and studying God's Word as you were when you first received Jesus. But just as a married couple's commitment to one another must continue steadfast long after the honeymoon ends, so our commitment to learn and apply God's Word must remain steadfast as we continue to grow as Christians.

As you develop mature, disciplined Bible study habits, you'll find it more rewarding and enriching even than your first love of Scripture.

Building a Good Foundation

Billy Graham has been asked many times, "If you had your ministry to do over, what would you change?" I've heard him answer, "I would study twice as much and preach half as much." That's good advice. We tend to underestimate the importance of a good biblical foundation for any ministry God calls us to undertake. It's easy as a Christian to get out there and start doing a lot of things for God. But it's wise to take time to get to know the God we are serving and proclaiming. And you can't really know God without knowing His Word.

Today's church tends to push celebrity converts into the limelight too soon. Whenever a sports hero, entertainment figure, or notorious criminal becomes a Christian, the first thing we want him or her to do is write a Christian book or cut a gospel record. We want to get his testimony in print or on tape even before he has much of a testimony to give. We want him on our Christian television programs. Then we want him in our churches telling everyone about his changed life and even giving the message.

The problem is, most of them aren't ready. Can you imagine someone putting you on the platform as a model Christian when you were only a month old in the Lord? If someone had done so with me, the church would have been in trouble. I didn't yet know which way was up. I knew my sin was forgiven, but I was young in my faith and ignorant of the Word of God.

When we elevate Christian celebrities too fast, we hurt them. The Bible warns us not to put a new convert in a position of authority, "lest being puffed up with pride he fall into the same condemnation as the devil" (1 Timothy 3:6).

But year after year new converts are lifted up and pushed into the limelight. Then we hear that one of them has fallen away because he didn't take time to get a good foundation.

You may not be a recently converted celebrity, but the principle is the same for you. The deeper your foundation in God's Word, the more stable will be your Christian life. The perfect example from the early church is Saul the persecutor who became Paul the apostle. Saul was a notable convert, a real celebrity in his day. We probably would have signed him to a book contract and a speaking tour as soon as the scales fell from his eyes. But the Lord was more interested in the long term. He wanted to make Saul into Paul, just as He had turned Simon into Peter.

He directed Paul to take time for study and preparation for his ministry. Paul went into the desert for three years and faded into obscurity (Galatians 1:15-18). More people need to follow his example. During Paul's three years in Arabia and Damascus, he built a strong foundation for his ministry by spending time with Jesus and, no doubt, the Old Testament Scriptures.

Similarly, every moment you spend in God's Word helps prepare you for God's plan for your life. As Alan Redpath said in *The Making of a Man of God*, "The salvation of a soul is the miracle of the moment. But the making of a man of God is the task of a lifetime." God is never in a hurry. He's building for eternity. What are a few months—or even years—when you keep your eye on eternity? Your consistent, daily attention to God's Word is essential to equipping you for what God calls you to do today and in the future.

Wisdom Through the Word

Look again at Stephen the martyr, whose brief story is found in Acts 6 and 7. He was one of seven men who had distinguished themselves in the young church as "of good reputation, full of the Holy Spirit and wisdom" (Acts 6:3). It's obvious that this young man was a great student of Scripture. Stephen was full of wisdom because he had an incredible grasp and understanding of God and His Word. His impassioned message recorded in Acts 7:2-53 is the longest of any preacher in the New Testament. In it he gives a detailed overview of the history of the nation of Israel and explains how it points to Jesus. God used Stephen's sermon to bring conviction to those who had spent their lives in the study of Scripture, yet had rejected the Messiah the Scriptures reveal.

Throughout the Bible we are told that God's Word is key to gaining wisdom. Notice in the following verses how wisdom is associated with personal involvement in God's Word:

- The law of the Lord is perfect, converting the soul; the testimony of the Lord is sure, making wise the simple (Psalm 19:7);

- The fear of the Lord is the beginning of wisdom; a good understanding have all those who do His commandments (Psalm 111:10);

- You, through your commandments, make me wiser than my enemies (Psalm 119:98);

- For the Lord gives wisdom; from His mouth come knowledge and understanding (Proverbs 2:6);

- The fear of the Lord is the beginning of wisdom, and the knowledge of the Holy One is understanding (Proverbs 9:10);

- Therefore whoever hears these sayings of Mine, and does them, I will liken to a wise man who built his house on the rock (Matthew 7:24).

The object of our Bible study is not to amass volumes of facts so we can amaze others with our knowledge. That was the mistake of the Jewish leaders who crucified Jesus, stoned Stephen, and persecuted the church. They had knowledge but no wisdom. They knew the details of Scripture but not the God of Scripture. Our goal in Bible study is to know, love, and obey God better every day. Only as we grow wise in the knowledge of God will we be equipped to meet the challenges of our troubled world.

Getting into the Word

"Okay, Greg," you may be saying, "I see the importance of being well grounded in God's Word. But how do I do it? What are some practical steps I can take to be assured that I am growing consistently in God's Word?"

Good question! Growing strong in God's Word doesn't happen by osmosis just because you have a dozen Bibles lying around your home and faithfully carry one to church every Sunday. You need to get into the Word personally and specifically if you want God's Word to get into you. Here are some practical, biblically based steps you can take to get into God's Word.

1. Study the Word. Second Timothy 2:15 reads, "Study to show thyself approved unto God, a workman that needeth not to be ashamed, rightly dividing the word of truth" (KJV). A lot of Christians *read* the Bible, but how many actually *study* the Bible? The word "study" means "make haste and exert yourself." The phrase "rightly dividing" means "dissecting correctly, cutting straight the word of truth." Studying the Bible means taking extra effort to make sure you are getting the message straight.

One way to study God's Word is to ask yourself specific questions as you read. Some people write down their responses to these questions so they have a running commentary of each passage for future reference. Here are some questions you might want to ask yourself as you open the Bible to study a passage:

- What is the main subject of the passage?
- Who are the people discussed in the passage?
- Who is speaking?
- About whom is this person speaking?
- What is the key verse in the passage?
- What does the passage teach me about Jesus?
- Is there a sin mentioned I need to confess or forsake?
- Is there a command I should obey?
- Is there a promise I need to claim?
- Is there a prayer recorded I might pray?

2. Meditate on the Word. Psalm 1:2 says that we are blessed if we delight in the law of the Lord and meditate on it day and night. Meditating on God's Word means to think about it, to slow down and chew on it mentally like a cow chews on her cud. You are better off reading five verses slowly and thoughtfully and understanding what they mean than you are reading five chapters quickly and not getting anything out of them. As you learn to slow down and contemplate each verse, you allow the Holy Spirit greater opportunity to speak to you through the passage you're studying.

3. Pray to understand the Word. Proverbs 2:3 instructs, "Cry out for discernment, and lift up your voice for understanding." In Psalm 119:18 the psalmist prays, "Open my eyes, that I may see wondrous things from Your law." If we are going to get the most out of the Scriptures we read, we must ask God to help us understand. Every time we open the Bible we need to pray something like, "Father, I believe You are the author of this Book. I believe, as You say, that all Scripture is breathed by You. Therefore, I ask You as the author to take me on a guided tour of Your Word today. Help me understand, and show me how these truths apply to my life." Your sincere prayer for guidance will cause the Bible to come alive during your time of study.

4. *Memorize the Word.* It is very important to commit Scripture to memory. Once Scripture is ingrained in your memory, it will always be there to use. The time will come when those verses will pay great dividends. They will bring comfort to your heart as well as needed strength in times of temptation. We're told in Psalm 119:11, "Your word I have hidden in my heart, that I might not sin against You." Although it is good to carry a Bible in your pocket, purse, or briefcase, the best place to carry it is in your heart!

Many wonderful Bible memorization plans are available these days; card packs for pocket or purse, page-a-day Scripture calendars, etc. The best way for me to remember something is to write it down. When I write it down, it is engraved more deeply in my memory, much deeper than if I merely read it. Writing Bible verses down seems to help the material enter my mind and gives it more "staying power."

It is also a good practice to keep a journal or notebook with your Bible. When a passage speaks to you, write down what God has shown you. Maybe it won't apply to you at that moment, but tomorrow, next week, or next month it may be just what you need.

Application Is the Goal

What's the ultimate goal of these and other Bible study strategies? To help us apply God's Word to our everyday actions and activities. God's Word must affect the way we live. It's not enough to go through the Word of God; God's

Word must go through you! It's not how you mark your Bible that counts; it's how your Bible marks you!

Is the Word affecting you that way? Is it sustaining your life? Is it controlling your thoughts, the way you conduct your business, your home life, and even your free time? It's only when we put ourselves under the authority of His Word and submit to its teaching that we become true, on-fire disciples of Jesus Christ.

Colossians 3:16 says, "Let the word of Christ dwell in you richly." Another way to say this would be, "Let Christ's words be perfectly at home in you." God wants His Word to permeate every area of your life. If you want your life to be on fire for God to the point that it impacts people around you, you need to fuel that blaze with consistent attention to God's Word.

CHAPTER FOUR

LOVING PEOPLE, LOVING GOD

A Thriving Christian Is a Loving Christian

Another valuable lesson we learn about these first-century believers is that they loved one another. We read that "they devoted themselves to fellowship" (Acts 2:42). An important word in the original language is used here for the word "fellowship." It is the Greek word *koinonia*. This word is so full of meaning it is translated a number of ways in the book of Acts. The words "fellowship," "communion," "distribution," "contribution," "partnership," and "partakership" are all used to express it.

The *koinonia* experience relates to many things. It speaks of the unique bond we experience as believers in our conversations and worship. But *koinonia* not only speaks of fellowship in worship; it also speaks of fellowship in giving. In fact, *koinonia* is the word Paul used for the collection he organized among the Greek churches for the needy in Jerusalem.

Jesus taught that it is more blessed to give than receive. True fellowship is not only telling our Christian friends that we love them, but also looking for tangible ways to show them our love. This trait should be the earmark of every believer who wants to turn his or her world rightside up. As Jesus said, "By this will all know that you are my disciples, if you have love for one another" (John 13:35).

This goes against the secular thinking of our day, where everyone wants "their rights." The slogan of the moment is "What about *my* needs?" We don't forgive anymore. We get revenge. We don't look for opportunities to serve. We seek to be served.

Yet a sign of real spiritual growth is when a believer realizes that going to church is not something he should do merely to be spiritually fed and built up. A believer is truly maturing when he realizes that going to church is also an opportunity to be sensitive to the needs of others. Jesus said, "The Son of Man did not come to be served, but to serve" (Matthew 20:28). Instead of sprinting to our car after the singing of the last song in a worship service, we should be praying, "Lord, now that I've heard your Word, please give me an opportunity to put it into action. Lead me to someone I can encourage, help, or pray for."

But I must warn you: If you start praying like that, you *will* get answers. So be ready, as Paul instructed Timothy, "in season and out of season" (2 Timothy 4:2).

Jesus said, "Give, and it will be given to you: good measure, pressed down, shaken together, and running over. . . . For with the same measure that you use, it will be measured back to you" (Luke 6:38). You may come to church with your "spiritual fuel tank" empty. But if you come to love, serve, and give to others, you will leave with your tank full! Instead of draining your spiritual resources, serving others will cause them to be replenished! Proverbs 11:25 echoes this, saying, "The generous soul will be made rich, and he who waters will also be watered himself."

On the last night Jesus spent with His disciples, the emphasis of His teaching was on loving servanthood. Jesus said, "By this all will know that you are My disciples, if you have love one for another" (John 13:35). One of the most powerful witnesses Christians have is the unmistakable act of compassion we demonstrate toward others. It speaks volumes and, in a sense, "it earns us the right" to preach the gospel to others.

Before I became a believer, I saw the love and concern the Christians on my high school campus had for one another. It made a deep impression on me. This was in the late '60s, and although the concepts of peace and love were widely proclaimed, I never saw it in anyone except these obviously committed Christians. It was this example that began to soften my hardened heart to the preaching of the gospel, leading to my acceptance of Jesus Christ as my Lord and Savior.

The church is made up of people just like you. Are you a loving believer? Do your actions live up to your words?

A Thriving Christian Is a Worshiping Christian

The third quality we find in the first-century church that transformed the world was that it was a worshiping church. Again in Acts 2:42 we read, "They devoted themselves . . . to the breaking of bread and to prayer" (NIV). Clearly this idea includes worship, for it is a definite form of prayer. Something wonderful and supernatural takes place when God's people gather together to worship Him. There is nothing like it anywhere in the world.

Recently I watched a video of a well-known rock performer singing a song that had become something of an anthem for his generation, the baby boomers. As the song began in the crowded stadium, thousands of Bic lighters were ignited, creating a starlike effect against the darkness.

As the people swayed in time to the song, singing the lyrics from memory, I was struck by the sadness of it all. Here was a generation who thought they would change their world. They believed their ideals and philosophies would really make a difference. But time marched on. Now they are past the age of 30, the very age of the people they said they could never trust.

As I watched the people in this video sing, I thought to myself, *This is as close as this world can get to worship.* It is only a shallow rendition of what true believers experience as we come together in that common bond of *koinonia.* True worship is not merely the singing of songs to God; it is the living of our lives in a way that pleases God. In fact, our singing and prayers are but the outward manifestations of a life lived daily for the glory of God.

Hebrews 13:15,16 gives us a good overview of the kind of worship God desires: "Therefore by Him let us continually offer the sacrifice of praise to God, that is, the fruit of our lips, giving thanks to His name. But do not forget to do good and to share, for with such sacrifices God is well-pleased."

Passionate worship of God is not just the singing of our songs, but also the sharing of our resources. It is not just the lifting of our hands in praise, but also the giving from our hands to others.

Our "sacrifice of praise to God" is something unique to us as Christians. No other religion "sings" like the Christian life. And we should cherish this. As Psalm 40:3 says, "He has put a new song in my mouth—praise to our God; many will see it and fear, and will trust in the Lord."

Not only was worship an active part of these early Christians' lives, but prayers of supplication and petition were vital as well. Next we will see just how important prayer is to a passionate Christian.

CHAPTER FIVE

$\mathcal{T}$HE POWER OF PRAYER

ONE CRUCIAL REASON the early Christians were so passionate in their faith and love for God was that they "continued steadfastly . . . in prayers" (Acts 2:42). The book of Acts reveals the indispensable nature of prayer in empowering the New Testament church. For example:

- The church was born as the followers of Jesus prayerfully waited for the power He promised them (1:12-14; 2:1-4);

- When persecution threatened to stamp out the infant church, believers went to prayer, then spoke God's Word with boldness (4:23-31);

- The growing church appointed additional leaders so the apostles could focus on prayer and preaching (6:1-4);

- In response to Peter's prayer, Tabitha was restored to life (9:36-43);

- The respective prayers of Cornelius and Peter resulted in the gospel being preached to Gentiles for the first time (10:1-48);

- Constant prayer by the church resulted in Peter being miraculously delivered from jail and possible execution (12:5-17);

- Missionaries were sent out and elders appointed with prayer and fasting (13:1-3; 14:21-23);

- Paul and Silas were miraculously delivered from jail, and the jailer and his family were converted, as a result of prayer (16:16-34).

The New Testament epistles, written to those first Christians and to us, persistently instruct believers to pray. Consider these verses:

- [Continue] steadfastly in prayer (Romans 12:12);

- Praying always with all prayer and supplication in the Spirit, being watchful to this end with all perseverance and supplication for all the saints (Ephesians 6:18);

- Be anxious for nothing, but in everything by prayer and supplication, with thanksgiving, let your requests be made known to God (Philippians 4:6);

- Continue earnestly in prayer, being vigilant in it with thanksgiving (Colossians 4:2);

- Pray without ceasing (1 Thessalonians 5:17).

While prayer was a way of life for the early church, many Christians today don't employ this powerful and effective weapon often enough. We are far quicker to protest than to pray. We are more ready to boycott than to believe that God can be strong on our behalf. It is essential that we understand how effective prayer can be in facing everyday problems, as well as the tragic and seemingly hopeless situations in our world.

Steadfast, Ceaseless Prayer

Prayer should be second nature to a child of God. That's the picture of prayer we have in the Scriptures: steadfast, constant, ceaseless, continuing, praying everywhere we go, praying about everything that happens. Prayer should be like breathing.

That reminds me of the time my wife and I taught our youngest son, Jonathan, to pray. It became almost second nature to him, and he almost never forgot! In fact, whenever we forgot to pray at mealtime, he brought it to our attention—but usually he waited until we started to eat, because he liked to catch us red-handed. So he waited until we took our first few bites and then said with obvious glee, "You forgot to pray!"

To this day, if you ask Jonathan to pray for something, he remembers it. I can think of certain things I've asked him to remember to pray for, and without fail he does. Prayer comes naturally to him. Perhaps Jesus had this very quality in mind when He said we must become like little children to enter the kingdom of God.

Principles of Prevailing Prayer

In order to identify some important principles to help us continue steadfast in effective prayer, let's take a closer look at one event from the book of Acts. At the beginning of Acts 12, wicked King Herod is persecuting the church, having already executed James the brother of John and imprisoned Peter. Peter had been in prison once before but had been miraculously released by an angel of the Lord (Acts 5:17-21). To prevent another escape, Herod locked Peter behind two gates, chained him to two guards, and surrounded him with 14 guards. By all human reasoning, there was no way Peter could get out.

What did Peter's fellow believers do about this seemingly impossible situation? We read that: "Peter was therefore kept in prison, but constant prayer was offered to God for him by the church" (Acts 12:5). The church could have done a lot of other things. They could have staged a protest. They could have picketed the prison. They could have flooded Herod's palace with letters. But instead they recognized the power of prayer. Though every prison door was locked shut, one door remained open: the door into the presence of God. So they began to pray for Peter's deliverance. And their prayers were effective. Why? I think the following principles will help us understand how we, like the early Christians, can lift effective prayers to God.

1. Pray to God. That's not nearly so obvious as you might think. Sometimes our prayers fail to honor Him as God. Instead, we think of Him as a divine Santa Claus to whom we bring a list of wants. Or we treat Him like our butler or maid by ordering Him to get us the things we need. Or we view Him as some kind of heavenly vending machine, thinking all we have to do is push the right buttons, recite little magic formulas, or claim certain verses and He is required to dispense whatever we want.

Sometimes we never think of God at all because we are all wrapped up in ourselves and our own needs and problems. Then we're like the self-absorbed Pharisee that Jesus described in the parable in Luke 18:9-14 who "prayed thus with himself." This man's prayers never got any higher than the ceiling because God was not involved in the process.

The first principle of prayer is to recognize who you're addressing. This is your Creator you're speaking to, so approach Him with reverence. Often when we approach God's throne in prayer we skip the formalities and just get down to business: "Hello, God, how are You? Now here's what I want." That's not prayer; that's reciting a shopping list.

Jesus gave us a model prayer in Matthew 6:9-13 we call the Lord's Prayer. It begins with an address of respect and reverence: "Our Father in heaven, hallowed be Your name." "Our Father" recognizes the intimacy of our relationship with Him. "In heaven" acknowledges His holiness. "Hallowed be Your name" expresses our reverence for Him. You don't have to say these words verbatim every time you pray. But enter into His presence with your own heartfelt words that express your love and reverence.

When we address God as God, it's also crucial to remember that our goal is to align our will with God's will. The Lord's Prayer clearly teaches this: "Your kingdom come. Your will be done on earth as it is in heaven." That is, "Lord, before a petition leaves my lips, I ask You to overrule it if it's outside Your will. I want Your will more than my own." Think about the request you are about to bring. Is it God's will? Granted, we can't always know the will of God. That's why we always pray as Jesus did in the garden of Gethsemane, "Not as I will, but as You will" (Matthew 26:39). But we are also promised in James 1:5 that God will provide the wisdom we need to understand His will if we ask Him for it.

Why is it so important to pray in His will? First John 5:14,15 says, "Now this is the confidence that we have in Him, that if we ask anything according to His will, He hears us. And if we know that He hears us, whatever we ask, we know that we have the petitions that we have asked of Him." That's a significant promise. You'll get what you ask for if you pray according to His will. So the key is to align yourself with God's will. Prayer is not bending God *your* way; prayer is bending you *His* way. Prayer is not overcoming God's reluctance; it's taking hold of His willingness. Prayer is not getting your will in heaven; it's getting God's will on earth. Nothing lies outside the reach of prayer except that which lies outside of the will of God.

Jesus had this in mind in John 15:7 when He said, "If you abide in Me, and My words abide in you, you will ask what you desire, and it shall be done for you." This verse could be literally translated, "If you are maintaining a living communion with Me, and My words are at home in your life, I command you to ask at once something for yourself, whatever your heart desires, and it will become yours."

Of course, most of us latch onto such a promise immediately. We like it. It excites us. Whatever my heart desires is mine! But sometimes we skip over the condition of the promise: *If* we maintain a living communion with Him and His Word is at home in us, *then* He will give us the desire of our heart. But if we are in communion with God and His Word is at home in us, our desires are going to change. We're not going to pray for frivolous, self-indulgent things. We're going to want what He wants for us, starting with a desire to become more like Him so we will love what He loves and hate what He hates. Therefore, when we ask for the desires of our heart, we will receive them.

2. Pray without ceasing. The second principle of prayer we learn from Acts 12:5 is that these early believers prayed without ceasing. "Constant prayer" was being offered for Peter. The phrase could also be translated, "they prayed with agony." They prayed with passion from the depths of their heart. They didn't throw up some casual, flippant request off the top of their head and then forget about it.

They agonized in prayer for Peter from the depths of their souls, and they did so until they got an answer.

Recognizing the urgency of the situation, the church probably prayed through the night. Note also that Peter was not released from prison until the night before his planned execution. So the church may have prayed continually for days or weeks.

In our fast-paced, busy lives, ceaseless, impassioned prayer is almost a lost art. Many of us race through our prayers as quickly as possible because we have somewhere to go, someone to see, or something to do. But usually we have time for the things we want to do, time that could be used for prayer.

When was the last time you turned off the TV for the evening and spent some time in prayer? If you really want God to use you to touch your community and your world, you must be willing to invest time in fervent prayer as the early Christians did.

3. Agree in prayer. The third principle of prevailing prayer in Acts 12:5 teaches us to pray in agreement with one another. Constant prayer was being offered to God for Peter's deliverance "by the church." These believers were acting on Jesus' promise in Matthew 18:19: "If two of you agree on earth concerning anything that they ask, it will be done for them by My Father in heaven."

This principle of prayer is often misunderstood. Suppose two people say, "Let's agree together and ask God to give us the island of Maui. Then we'll split up the island. You can take the south and I'll take the north." Will God give them what they want? Not likely. Jesus' promise doesn't mean that you can pick out anything you want and then find someone to agree with you so God is bound to do what you ask. Rather, it's saying that if two people *with the same God-given burden* are sure of His will and in agreement with the Spirit of God and with one another, God will grant their request. There is great power when same-minded people agree in prayer!

4. Pray even when you doubt. This principle for prayer may not be as commendable as the first three, but it's vital that you know it. It's okay to pray when you still have doubts about how God is going to answer. The group of believers praying for Peter prayed to God, prayed ceaselessly, and prayed in agreement—but quite honestly, they also prayed with some doubt that Peter would be delivered.

Peter was sleeping on the night of his deliverance. That's amazing since James had already been killed by Herod and Peter was to go to trial the next day. He was probably the only Christian in Jerusalem sleeping that night. Everybody else was awake praying and worrying about him. But Peter's sleep didn't last long, for God sent an angel to his dark prison cell to wake him up. Miraculously, Peter's chains fell off, the doors opened automatically, and he walked out a free man.

Peter then went to the house where the Christians were praying for his deliverance and knocked on the door. I can see it now. The spiritual leaders were in the back room, most likely praying something like, "Oh God, deliver our brother Peter! Lord, we love him. We want to see him again. Just bring him back to us. We know you can do it!"

Suddenly, they heard a knock at the door. "What is that distraction? Father, we just . . ."

They heard another knock. A young girl named Rhoda quietly went to answer and then excitedly ran back to the room and interrupted their prayer. "What is it?" they asked impatiently.

"Peter is standing on the front porch!" she replied.

"You're crazy!" they said. Then they picked up where they left off, "Oh God, deliver Peter." I'll bet their mouths dropped down to their knees when they finally saw him.

I don't think I'm taking liberties with this story. The account in Acts 12 certainly implies that the disciples didn't believe God had answered their prayer. Yet despite their doubts, their prayer was mightier than Herod and mightier than hell.

Help My Unbelief

Faith is clearly a scriptural requirement for effective prayer. No doubt we have hindered the hand of God by our unbelief on many occasions. Nonetheless, if you are a little weak in the faith department, God can still work on your behalf with what you offer Him.

This certainly is not taught to us by the positive confession, name-it-and-claim-it crowd. They say, "If you claim it and believe it, then you'll have it. If you don't have it, it's because you lack faith."

Such a position brings an enormous amount of heartache and guilt to needy people. Let's say that Bill is terminally ill and the doctors hold no hope for his recovery. Then Bob comes in and says, "God wants to heal you, Brother Bill. We're going to pray right now and you're going to be healed."

So Bill and Bob pray. But what if Bill remains ill? "Those are just the symptoms," Bob says. "God has healed you. Take it by faith and get out of bed right now."

Bill gets out of bed only to find that he's not ready to get out. "It's just a lack of faith," his well-meaning but misguided friend says. "Don't look to those things. Just believe God."

As time passes, however, Bill doesn't get better. In fact, he gets worse. Assessing the situation, Bob says, "It's your lack of faith, Bill. If you just had more faith, God would heal you."

This is wrong and unscriptural! True, the Bible says that God works in response to faith. But it also asserts that God sometimes works despite our lack of faith. The following scenarios show four different levels of faith and how God responded to each of them.

1. Sincere faith. Consider the woman described in Luke 8:43-48 who had a serious illness for 12 years. She believed if she could just touch Jesus, she would be healed.

One day her opportunity came. Jesus was moving through town, surrounded by throngs of excited people. As Jesus and the multitude surged down the road, the woman pressed in, reached through, and touched the edge of His robe. Suddenly God's healing power bolted through her body and she was cured instantaneously.

Jesus stopped in His tracks and asked, "Who touched Me?"

The disciples said, "Who touched You? Who *didn't* touch You? Everyone's grabbing and pulling You, trying to get close to You."

Jesus said, "I perceived power going out from Me." The woman bowed down before Him and told her story. Jesus didn't reprove her. Instead He commended her for her faith.

Yes, your faith can and does play a significant part in meeting your needs. But sometimes God responds to the faith of someone else when our own faith is weak.

2. Another's faith. Matthew 8:5-13 tells the story of the Roman centurion and his servant, who was deathly ill. The centurion came to Jesus and said, "Speak a word, and my servant will be healed."

Jesus answered, "Go your way; and as you have believed, so let it be done for you." And the centurion's servant was healed. In this case, God honored the faith of the centurion on behalf of his servant.

If I was sick and didn't have enough faith to believe for my healing, I would look around for others who would exercise their faith on my behalf. Even when our faith is weak, God can still meet our needs through the faith of another as He did for the servant through the centurion's faith.

3. Weak faith. Sometimes the Lord grants our prayers even when our faith is minuscule. This truth is underscored in the story in Mark 9:14-29 of the man who brought his demon-possessed son to Jesus and asked for help. Jesus responded, "If you believe, all things are possible to him who believes."

The man exclaimed, "Lord, I believe; help my unbelief!"

Did Jesus respond, "I'm sorry, but that won't do. You have to speak it into existence. You have to name it and claim it"? Of course not! He honored the man's faith, as weak as it was, and delivered his son from the demon.

I believe God will honor your prayer when you come to Him and say, "Lord, with as much faith as I have, I believe. But if there is any doubt standing in the way of my prayer being answered, help my unbelief."

Look at Acts 12. Here was the church praying to God for Peter, praying fervently, and praying constantly, yet they doubted. When God answered their prayer, they couldn't believe it.

We've done that, haven't we? Haven't you been shocked when God actually answered your prayer? What does that show? It shows that God loves us and makes allowances for our struggling faith. This doesn't mean unbelief is a commendable virtue. We should seek to grow in faith day by day. But in the meantime, if you are honest to God and say, "Lord, I believe; help my unbelief," you can move forward from there.

4. *Divine intervention.* The story of Lazarus being raised from the dead in John 11:38-44 illustrates how God can work despite a total lack of faith. Certainly, Lazarus didn't have a lot going for him in the faith department. He was dead. Yet Jesus raised him from the grave. Was it because of the faith of his sisters, Mary and Martha? No way. They even accused Jesus of failing them by not coming soon enough to heal their brother while he was still alive. Did Jesus respond to the faith of the mourners? Far from it. They were so filled with unbelief it drove Jesus to tears.

Lazarus was raised from the dead because Jesus directly intervened in his hopeless situation. This gives us confidence that when no one around us has much faith—including ourselves—God can still respond to our prayers and meet our needs. Why? Because He is God and chooses to intervene out of His great love for us.

God's Work and Our Responsibility

Notice in Acts 12:10 that as soon as Peter was outside the prison, the angel disappeared and Peter was left to get to Mary's house on his own. The angel could have airlifted him to the house and dropped him right into the room, but he didn't. In response to prayer, God took care of the impossible and left the possible to Peter.

Yes, there is a place for miracles, but there is also a place for our own efforts. Only Jesus could raise Lazarus from the dead, but someone else had to loose him from his grave clothes. Only Jesus could multiply five loaves and two fish to feed 5000, but someone else had to distribute the food and pick up the leftovers. Sometimes we ask for miracles when God just wants us to take practical steps.

Let's say you have a job but you don't want to go to work this week because you're not in the mood. You'd rather stay home and watch television. So you don't work all week long. You call in sick every day even though you're feeling fine. Then at the end of the week you don't get a paycheck. As a result, you become hungry. So you begin to pray, "Oh God, send me food. Oh Lord, I know You can do it. Lord, You provided for Elijah, and I just pray You'll provide for me even as You did for him."

But no food comes. Why not? Because you don't need a miracle; you need to go to work! You're praying for a miracle, but you're violating biblical principles in the process. The Scripture teaches, "If anyone shall not work, neither shall he eat" (2 Thessalonians 3:10). If you have the ability and the opportunity to work and you don't do so because you just don't feel like it, it's your own fault when you don't receive the material things you need.

On the other hand, sometimes we try to do what only God can do. Suppose you pray for an unsaved friend to come to Christ. But then you think, *God needs my help. Some high-pressure witnessing tactics should do the job.* So you start badgering your friend to repent and believe, thinking God can't save him without your "help."

The result? You end up complicating the process. Do your part by being a loving, caring friend, sharing the gospel when God provides the opportunity, inviting your friend to church, and praying fervently. Then allow God to do what only He can do.

Acts 12 opens with James dead, Peter in prison, and Herod triumphing. The chapter closes with Herod dead, Peter free, the Word of God triumphing, and the church revived and filled with a holy passion and zeal. What made the difference? Prayer. You need to keep this truth in mind each day. Sometimes things can look pretty bleak, but keep praying! See what God will do over the long term in response to your faithful prayers.

CHAPTER SIX

$\mathcal{F}$AITHFUL TO THE FINISH

I WAS 18 YEARS OLD AND HAD been a Christian for almost a year when I first felt the call of God to preach and teach. One day I went into the office of my pastor, Chuck Smith. I took a seat in front of his desk and blurted out, "Chuck, God has called me into the ministry. I believe He wants me to preach the gospel and teach the Word of God."

"That's great, Greg," Chuck said with a knowing smile, leaning back in his chair. I fully expected next to hear something like, "Listen, Greg, Sunday morning sounds good to me. Why don't you just preach in my place this week!" But instead he said, "Greg, I want you to talk to one of the pastors on staff here. His name is Romaine."

Pastor L.E. Romaine is a wonderful man of God. I didn't know it at the time, but he often runs interference for Chuck Smith. A former Marine Corps sergeant, Romaine has taken countless young bucks like me and whipped us into shape using some of the same tactics he used in the Marines. I eagerly bounded into Pastor Romaine's office, confident I could do just about anything he set before me.

Romaine looked me over like a drill sergeant eyeing a raw recruit. "I'll tell you what, young man," he said. "I've got just the job for you." I visualized a great preaching opportunity or a chance to lead a Bible study or even counsel someone. But he didn't give me a Bible and a place to preach; he handed me a broom and a place to sweep! And for the next several weeks I ministered faithfully to a large pepper tree that dropped a new batch of leaves as soon as I had swept up the old ones.

What a letdown! I had envisioned crowds of spiritually hungry people waiting for my profound insights from Scripture. I had imagined troubled individuals seeking out seasoned counsel from my one-year experience of knowing Jesus. Instead I swept leaves.

Weeks later Chuck and Romaine apparently saw the light and decided to give me a new responsibility. I was summoned to the office and eagerly awaited my preaching, teaching, or counseling assignment. But I was disappointed again. My next grand mission was to purchase a new doorknob for the church office. Still, I was grateful for the opportunity to do something other than sweep leaves.

On my way to the department store I felt as if I was on a mission for God. I could not fail! It seemed a simple enough task—until I arrived at the doorknob section of the hardware department. I had never seen so many doorknobs in my life. They came in all sizes, shapes, and finishes. I paced back and forth, deciding and then changing my mind. Finally, I made my selection and proudly brought it back to the church office.

It was the wrong size. Deflated but determined, back to the store I went.

In the next several months I was given many similar opportunities to serve the Lord. I learned to do them, not as jobs, but as ministries to the Lord. Eventually I was asked to make hospital calls and lead Bible studies. Before long I was the leader of a small Bible study group that eventually became Harvest Christian Fellowship, the church I pastor today.

I admit that during those first days of my "ministry" I was tempted to sneak into the church yard at night and chop down that worthless pepper tree. But now I treasure the memories of those days sweeping leaves and running errands. I recognize that God, through the wisdom of my pastors at Calvary Chapel, was building in me a quality that has helped keep my passion for the Lord burning for more than 27 years. In fact, even though we don't have a pepper tree at Harvest, we utilize the same principles for preparing people for ministry I learned from Pastor Chuck Smith and Pastor L.E. Romaine in Costa Mesa.

Your Faithful Servant

The quality I'm talking about is faithfulness. As an 18-year-old, brand-new Christian, my enthusiasm for the ministry was strong. I was ready to preach to thousands and attempt great feats for God. But pastors Chuck and Romaine weren't all that impressed by my fervor. They'd seen scores of young men like me chomping at the bit to get behind a pulpit or take over a Bible study. What they were looking for was someone who would be faithful, even in little things like sweeping leaves and buying doorknobs.

The hallmark of the passionate believers of the first century was faithfulness. The two most prominent apostles in the early church made it clear that faithfulness is the essential quality of the Christian life. Paul wrote, "Moreover it is required in stewards that one be found faithful" (1 Corinthians 4:2). And Peter instructed us, "Each one should use whatever gift he has received to serve others, faithfully administering God's grace in its various forms" (1 Peter 4:10, NIV).

Christians who are faithful in the little things can be used by God to accomplish great things. Think about Stephen for a moment. Here was a man of good reputation, full of the Holy Spirit and wisdom, but the disciples had him waiting on tables and distributing food and clothing to a bunch of gripers. Stephen could have protested, "Excuse me, but I think I have a higher calling on my life. I feel called to preach and teach, and I have a miracle ministry as well. Don't you realize that I'm too important for this kind of menial service?"

But that's not what Stephen did. He started where God called him. Ultimately, we read of his powerful preaching and the miracles Jesus performed through his life. Similarly, if you want to be a person whom God will use, you must be faithful in the small areas. If you are not faithful there, don't expect God to give you more.

The early church made a significant impact on its world, not because it was made up of great people, but because it was made up of faithful people. Faithful to the Lord, faithful to the ministry, faithful in menial tasks, and faithful in great tasks. We look back today at the great men and women of God listed in the book of Acts and marvel at what they accomplished for God. But think of the thousands—perhaps tens of thousands—of unnamed believers over that 30-year span who quietly and faithfully served God and shared Jesus with their hurting world. If those early believers hadn't been faithful, who knows if you or I would be following Jesus today?

Some of us may aspire to be great missionaries for God. We yearn to cross the seas and convert people in faraway lands. But let me ask you: Have you started by crossing the street to share your faith? Does going to a foreign land make you a great missionary? If you won't share your faith right now, do you think something magical or mystical is going to happen as soon as you set foot on foreign soil? No, you need to start where you are now. You must be faithful with what God has set before you at this time in your life. And if you are, only He knows what opportunities will open up for you in the days ahead.

You can never be too small for God to use, but you can be too big. If you start thinking you're God's gift to humanity, you're going to fall, and fall hard. In a deluded moment you may begin to see yourself as indispensable to the work of God. If so, you're on thin ice. Scripture clearly and repeatedly warns against pride and arrogance. Although it's true that God has chosen to work through us, it is certainly not out of necessity. God doesn't *need* us; He uses us because He loves us and desires to include us in His work.

God could not have made this more plain than He did in Psalm 50:9-12: "I have no need of a bull from your stall or of goats from your pens, for every animal of the forest is mine, and the cattle on a thousand hills. I know every bird in the mountains, and the creatures of the field are mine. If I were hungry I would not tell you, for the world is mine, and all that is in it."

Or if that's not enough for you, consider the words of the apostle Paul in Athens: "The God who made the world and everything in it is the Lord of heaven and earth and does not live in temples built by hands. And he is not served by human hands, as if he needed anything, because he himself gives all men life and breath and everything else" (Acts 17:24,25, NIV).

When the eminent preacher C.H. Spurgeon was a young man, he was caught up in the great and mighty things God had in store for him. But the Lord brought him back to reality with this verse: "Do you seek great things for yourself? Do not seek them" (Jeremiah 45:5). Spurgeon stopped seeking greatness and focused instead on God's glory and being faithful to Him. Ultimately, God used him as one of the greatest preachers in modern church history. Like the first-century believers, Spurgeon learned the indispensable lesson of being faithful where God called him.

I have come to realize that God can easily get His work done without me. It is a privilege and an honor to be used as His instrument. Any success I enjoy in ministry is certainly not because of my skills or abilities; it's because of His power working in me. If I forget that, my words will fall to the ground and have no impact. The same is true of you in your ministry for Him. It is only when He is working through us that we are effective. God help us all to remain humble and usable to Him, for "God resists the proud, but gives grace to the humble" (James 4:6).

Running to Finish, Running to Win

It appears that the apostle Paul was something of a sports fan. Throughout his teaching he uses the vivid image of a runner to illustrate his determination and persistence as a faithful servant of Christ. In Acts 20:24, he says, "But none of these things move me; nor do I count my life dear to myself, so that I may finish my race with joy, and the ministry which I received from the Lord Jesus, to testify to the gospel of the grace of God." In Philippians 2:16, he states that he is "holding forth the word of life, so that I may rejoice in the day of Christ that I have not run in vain."

In Philippians 3:13,14 he continues the analogy: "Brethren, I do not count myself to have apprehended; but one thing I do, forgetting those things which are behind and reaching forward to those things which are ahead, I press toward the goal for the prize of the upward call of God in Christ Jesus." Paul likens himself to a runner in the last lap of the race, straining every muscle as he reaches out to the finish line. He refuses the temptation to look back, lest it break his momentum.

In 1 Corinthians 9:24, the apostle applies the same image to all believers: "Do you not know that those who run in a race all run, but one receives the prize? Run in such a way that you may obtain it." Later, in writing to the church in Galatia, he picks up the analogy again. Rebuking believers for allowing false teachers to side-track them with a message of hyper-legalism, Paul writes, "You ran well. Who hindered you from obeying the truth?" (Galatians 5:7). Furthermore, the author of Hebrews, who might well have been Paul, writes, "Since we are surrounded by so great a cloud of witnesses, let us lay aside every weight, and the sin which so easily ensnares us, and let us run with endurance the race that is set before us" (Hebrews 12:1).

Paul's teaching and example call us not only to be faithful in this life, but to remain faithful until we cross the finish line. Sometimes we look at others who have started to follow the Lord but have fallen away, and we wonder if we will remain faithful until we reach the finish line. But I ask you: Do you want to finish joyfully and victoriously? If you do, then you will, because God wants you to do just that.

You are not running alone. Jesus is there with you. He is even more committed to your success than you are. The Bible says that Jesus is the author and finisher of your faith (Hebrews 12:2). It also says that He will complete the good work He began in you (Philippians 1:6). The Lord is prepared to finish what He has started in you, but He would appreciate a little cooperation on your part! If you continue to yield to His Spirit and obey His Word, you will finish with flying colors—and, in Peter's words, will "receive a rich welcome into the eternal kingdom of our Lord and Savior Jesus Christ" (2 Peter 1:11, NIV).

Going the Distance

The Christian life is a long-distance run, not a 50-yard dash. We're not called merely to be faithful while we're young and strong and healthy or while life is going well for us or for 20 or 30 years until we "retire." We're called to be passionate, fervent believers *for life*. Serving Jesus requires diligence. It requires perseverance. It requires discipline. We don't like to hear these words much, but they are a necessary part of our vocabulary if we want to finish the race.

I was a good runner in high school, but only for short distances. I could beat most people in the 50-yard dash, but I wasn't as strong in long-distance running. I always got winded and was unable to finish the race. Whenever I ran anything longer than a quarter mile, I would blast off from the starting line and leave everyone in my dust. But about the second or third lap, everyone would start passing me. By the time the race was over, small children, turtles, even inanimate objects were passing me. My problem was trying to run long-distance races with a short-distance mind-set. I didn't pace myself.

Many new Christians seem to explode off the starting line with great enthusiasm for serving God. They read their Bibles and pray with great fervor. They're either in church or a Bible study every night of the week. They witness to all their friends. But when the first rush of excitement wears off, their spiritual legs begin to wobble. They can't seem to do all they want to do for God, so they feel like failures. People let them down, temptations get them down, and discouragement fills their heart. The race has just begun, but they're out of gas and ready to quit.

We need to help new Christians realize that an enthusiastic start is wonderful, but the race is won on faithfulness. We need to help them learn to hang in there faithfully despite the hurdles of disappointment, temptation, and discouragement that cause them to wonder if they should have stayed at the starting line.

When we begin to feel winded and long to collapse in the shade somewhere off the track, we must keep our eyes focused on the "world record holder" for this event. Hebrews 12:2 says, "Looking unto Jesus, the author and finisher of our faith, who for the joy that was set before Him endured the cross, despising its shame, and has sat down at the right hand of the throne of God." When the race gets tough, we must remember that Jesus not only showed us how to endure faithfully (in a much tougher race than ours, by the way), but by His Spirit He lives in us to keep our spiritual passion alive until we cross the finish line.

The Joy of Running

Avid runners tell me that after you run for a certain period of time you reach a kind of euphoric state. It's called "runner's high." I have yet to discover this personally. I only reach greater states of pain. Over the years I have tried to get into running, but I admit I don't enjoy it. I always start off with a bang. I get a pair of good running shoes and hit the course a few times. But then, after feeling the aches and pains, I give up. I can't say that I equate my running with joy.

Paul wanted to be among the company of those who finished the race with joy. He knew it required discipline. He knew it could be painful at times. But he also knew the joy of running well and finishing strongly despite the obstacles and pain.

In our faithful service to Christ there is joy in the midst of all the pain and discouragement we might face. What is the joy? It's the joy that comes from knowing who we are running for and who we are running with. The fact that

Jesus is our ever-present source of strength, our example of righteousness, and our goal makes the hard work and rigorous discipline worth it.

Knowing that Jesus is watching us keeps us going. Knowing that we will stand before Him one day makes us want to finish well. We are not competing with others, so we should avoid the temptation to compare ourselves with one another or to run for someone else's approval. We must run for Christ. People will let us down. But if we fix our eyes on Jesus, He will keep us going.

Some years ago my son Christopher, a good runner, was in a track meet and my wife and I went to cheer him on. After the race the announcer said over the loud speaker, "All right, you dads, now it's your opportunity to get out there and run. We're going to let all the fathers have a big race against each other."

I thought, *The glory days are here again!* I casually walked out to the track, feeling smug that I just happened to be wearing my good running shoes. I began sizing up the competition—a bunch of dads with big bellies hanging over their belts—and thought, *I'll leave 'em all in my dust. I'll win easily. No problem.*

They fired the starting gun and we took off. But after only a few strides the pot-bellied dads started passing me. One, two, three, four, five, six—all of them were suddenly in front of me. I couldn't believe it. I was just getting started and pain was already wracking my body. So as we ran past a tree, I nonchalantly slowed down and walked off the track as though I never really intended to run the race. I was humiliated and in pain, so I quit.

I hope to do better in the race of life, with God's help. Exploding off the starting line may be impressive, but it's fruitless if we flame out and give up before reaching the finish line. Paul's emphasis was faithful, consistent ministry to Christ and others from beginning to end. I want to make his emphasis mine. There are no gold medals for blazing starts, only for gutsy finishes. I want to finish what I have begun and hear those golden words, "Well done, good and faithful servant."

People with a passion and zeal for God are people fueled by the power of the Spirit, tied into Jesus by the Word, worship, fellowship, and prayer, and committed to a lifetime of faithful service. This type of passion for God cannot be kept "inside." It is meant to be shared. Wherever we go, we should "sanctify the Lord in [our] hearts . . . always [being] ready to give a defense to everyone who asks you a reason for the hope that is in you" (1 Peter 3:15).

That was God's intention for the church from the beginning: "You shall receive power when the Holy Spirit has come upon you; and you shall be witnesses to Me" (Acts 1:8).

God has called you to reflect His righteousness and proclaim His love to a world in desperate need. You were not designed to be hidden under a basket, but to blaze brightly and give light to all who are around you (Matthew 5:14-16). It's only as God's fire ignites the hearts of those you touch for Him that you have any hope of seeing your world turned rightside up for the Lord.

But how is this accomplished? What must you understand about God's plan to reach your world in order to fully cooperate with Him and see it begin to happen? Part Two will offer some helpful answers.

PART TWO

SHARING
THE
PASSION

CHAPTER SEVEN

*D*IVINE
APPOINTMENTS IN
DAILY ROUTINE

PETER AND JOHN WERE ON THEIR way to the temple one afternoon to pray. It was another ordinary day. Neither heard an audible voice from heaven telling them to go to the temple, nor do we read of an angel from heaven directing them. They just happened to be going to the temple to pray as they usually did. But on this ordinary day God was about to do something extraordinary through these two on-fire disciples (see Acts 3:1-10).

On their way to the temple they passed by the gate called Beautiful, so named because of its splendor. This huge, Corinthian-style, bronze gate with gold and silver inlays led to the temple from the Court of the Gentiles. A flurry of activity always surrounded the gate. It was a perfect place for merchants to conduct business, and (as some commentators estimate) as many as 10,000 people would gather in the temple area during the time of prayer.

The milling crowds also made the temple gate a strategic place for the poor to beg. Apparently one of the fixtures at this ornate gate was a man who had been crippled from birth. He waited by the gate each day, hoping that worshipers would feel compelled to give him a little financial assistance.

When Peter and John came walking through the gate, the crippled man asked them for money. It's likely they had seen him there before. But today was different. God wanted to do a work not only in this poor man's life, but also in the lives of these two disciples.

Looking straight at the man, Peter said, "Silver and gold I do not have, but what I do have I give you: In the name of Jesus Christ of Nazareth, rise up and walk" (Acts 3:6). Peter then took the man by the hand and pulled him up. Supernatural strength bolted into those once-lifeless limbs and the man lame from birth not only took the first steps of his life, but in jubilant, heartfelt thanks, began to leap and praise God. The watching crowd was awestruck by this unexpected miracle.

It took a lot of boldness to do what Peter did. How would you have felt being in Peter's sandals? Here you are in the crowded temple courtyard surrounded by unbelievers just waiting for an excuse to ridicule you and your Christian faith. Then suddenly the Holy Spirit directs you to proclaim a lifelong cripple healed in the name of Jesus, and you pull him to his feet to prove it really happened. Would you be ready to go for broke on such a daring step of faith? Peter was. Not only that, he seized the moment and preached a powerful, hard-hitting message to the amazed crowd, and about 5000 people believed (Acts 3:11–4:4).

Extraordinary Living on Ordinary Days

Little did Peter and John know when they woke up that morning that a wildfire of ministry was going to spread through Jerusalem simply because they had a passion for

God and were available to serve Him. They were merely going through their daily routine when God revealed a divine appointment. And because these two disciples were alert to the Holy Spirit, an ordinary stroll to the temple turned into an extraordinary opportunity for spreading the gospel.

As I look back on my own life, I can see how God has often led me into extraordinary opportunities for ministry through ordinary means. I'm not talking about events quite as dramatic as the one Peter and John experienced. I'll be honest with you; I normally don't have the faith to pull crippled people out of wheelchairs. But I believe that if God wanted to do such a miracle through me or you, He would give us the faith to believe Him for it.

Yet God often brings someone across my path He wants me to touch for Him in the middle of my daily routine. He doesn't usually lead me into these situations by visions from heaven. And I've never had a prophet knock on my door and tell me my agenda for the day. I often discover God's divine appointment while running a simple errand.

Once I was in a department store looking for a pair of socks when nature called. I went into the restroom and found a stall. After a few moments I was startled to hear the voice of the man in the stall next to me say, "Were you supposed to meet me here?"

I thought, *What on earth is this all about?* Then I responded, "Not that I know of."

He then asked, "Do you have something for me?"

At this point my curiosity awakened. "What is it you are waiting for?"

"Some drugs."

"No, I don't have any drugs for you, but I have something far better."

He quickly responded, "What's that?"

"A personal relationship with Jesus Christ." At this point the absurdity of the situation struck me. Here I was, sitting in a public restroom talking to a stranger in the stall next to me and sharing the gospel. I wondered if God was having a little fun while directing my steps in such an unconventional way.

"I used to go to church," the man responded. "But I don't anymore."

"Where did you go to church?" I inquired, trying to get an idea of his spiritual background.

"Harvest Christian Fellowship."

I couldn't believe it! Here was a guy who had attended the church I've pastored for 20 years, trying to buy drugs from me. Talk about the Lord making it hard for a person to go the wrong direction!

"Do you know who I am?" I asked.

"No."

"I'm Greg Laurie, the pastor of Harvest Christian Fellowship!"

He was shocked, to say the least.

I told him that the Lord must really love him to send the pastor of his former church to the stall next to him when he was trying to make a drug buy. I asked him to meet me outside and I had the privilege of leading this young prodigal back to the Lord right there in the store's sock department.

I didn't hear an audible voice telling me, "Go into the restroom at the department store, take a seat, and I'll tell you what to do." I was just walking through my day and was thrilled to find myself smack dab in the middle of God's will. That's why it's important to commit your way to the Lord each day. The Bible says, "The steps of a good man are ordered by the Lord" (Psalm 37:23). So as you commit your way to the Lord, ask Him to lead you in the decisions you will face each day, and be ready for the divine appointments He brings your way.

The Transforming Power of Jesus

The religious leaders who heard Peter's sermon at the temple gate did not have the same response as the 5000 who believed. At this time, two main religious groups existed in Judaism: the Pharisees and the Sadducees. The Sadducees rejected the idea of the resurrection of the dead, believing that when you die you simply cease to exist. Considering this bleak outlook, that's why the Sadducees were "sad, you see." It is truly sad when a person doesn't have hope of life beyond the grave.

The Sadducees bristled when Peter proclaimed that Jesus had died and risen from the grave. So they ordered the temple police to arrest Peter and John and bring them before the Jewish ruling body, the Sanhedrin. Ironically, the two disciples found themselves standing before the very men who had been responsible for the crucifixion of their Lord. I can almost hear the authorities saying, "You know, this all seems very familiar. Didn't we just deal with this same problem a few months ago? These two men behave and sound just like that Nazarene carpenter we crucified."

Peter didn't waste this divine appointment either. He boldly informed the Jewish leaders that the healing of the crippled man had been accomplished through the name of Jesus Christ, whom they crucified. Even though the authorities were less than enamored with Peter and John's actions and words, they couldn't ignore the passion within them: "When the Council saw the boldness of Peter and John, and could see that they were obviously uneducated nonprofessionals, they were amazed and realized what being with Jesus had done for them!" (Acts 4:13, TLB).

I wonder if people can make the same observation about you and me when God arranges a divine appointment in the daily routine of our lives. What does this statement say to us about our witness to the people we contact every day? I think there are at least two important truths here to grasp.

1. *God uses ordinary people.* The Jewish leaders were amazed at what being with Jesus had done for mere "common folk." When the passage describes Peter and John as "uneducated," it doesn't mean that they were without basic education. But they hadn't been trained in theology in the rabbinical schools of the day. They didn't speak in the language of the theologian; they spoke in the vernacular of common people. They didn't walk around in special priestly robes; they dressed in ordinary clothes. Yet they captured the people's attention with their obvious knowledge, understanding, and insight into Scripture. The Council recognized that they were ordinary people doing extraordinary things.

When it comes to spreading the gospel, I've found that ordinary people are often more effective than the so-called "professionals." Many people do not want to listen to some preacher standing behind a pulpit. They want to hear from you. They can more easily identify with you because you work with them or live in their neighborhood and they know they can talk with you. For that reason you may reach people far more effectively than an astute theologian.

Maybe God hasn't called you to be a pastor, an evangelist, or a missionary. But He *has* called you to be an instrument He can use. Second Chronicles 16:9 says, "For the eyes of the Lord run to and fro throughout the whole earth, to show Himself strong on behalf of those whose heart is loyal to Him." In other words, God is looking for ordinary people through whom He can accomplish extraordinary feats.

Throughout the Bible we see God using common men and women, boys and girls. He used David, a shepherd boy, to lead the nation of Israel, bypassing more "qualified" people in the process. He called a frightened, young man like Gideon to become a brave man of valor. He used a simple girl named Esther to save the Jewish people from genocide, and a brave woman named Deborah to lead the armies of Israel when no man had the courage.

And in the book of Acts He used the former sometimes cowardly Simon Peter and the sometimes impatient John to be His spokespersons in building the early church. In fact, most of the men and women God employed in the book of Acts were no more "qualified" for spreading the gospel than you or I. These "heroes of the faith" had weaknesses as well as strengths, just like you and I have. Yet the same Holy Spirit working in their lives also works in yours, and what God did through them He can do through you. Remember, the book of Acts is a record "of all that Jesus *began* both to do and teach" (Acts 1:1, emphasis added). He wants to continue performing today through ordinary people just as He did in the first decades of the church.

2. God empowers our witness. The religious leaders knew that Peter and John had been with Jesus because of their unrestrained boldness. No doubt these authorities knew about Peter. They might well have heard about his denial of Jesus in the high priest's courtyard. Now, as Peter and John stood before them, they probably whispered to each other, "Isn't this the guy who denied the carpenter three times? Look at him now. He's an altogether different person!"

They saw in Peter and John the same boldness they witnessed in Jesus when He stood before the Sanhedrin during His trial. Because Jesus' disciples had been with Him, in many ways they had become like Him. Jesus' nature had become Peter and John's nature. How did this happen? It did not come about so much by *imitation* as by *impartation.*

They did not have to try or force it!

Abide in Jesus, spend time getting to know him and you won't have to consciously try to imitate him or become like him?

90 ∞ GREG LAURIE

Jesus best illustrated this process in John 15:5 when He said, "I am the vine, you are the branches." The branch of a grapevine conforms so much to the appearance of the vine you can hardly distinguish where one leaves off and the other begins. The branch draws its resources and strength from the vine and, as it conforms to the vine, brings forth the fruit. Likewise, God's goal and design for Christians is to be conformed to His image. Romans 8:29 says, "For whom He foreknew, He also predestined to be conformed to the image of His Son." God wants the nature of Jesus to become your nature, His goals to become your goals, His likes to become your likes, His dislikes to become your dislikes. The more we become like Him, the more pleasing we are to Him.

Have you ever noticed how two people who have been married to each other for a long time are so much like each other? They may have some of the same facial expressions or behavior traits. One of them can start a statement and the other can finish it. After awhile you just think of them as one.

That's how our walk and relationship with Jesus Christ ought to be. Look to yourself. Are you becoming more like Jesus as each year passes? Between the time you became a believer and now there should be a marked improvement in every facet of your life. Being a Christian is being more like Jesus, because we have been with Him.

Living Proof

The religious leaders had another problem besides having to face the convicting message about Christ once again in the message of Peter and John: They had to explain the beggar who had been miraculously touched by God. There seemed no way to refute this miracle, because the former cripple they all knew from the temple gate now leaped around for all to see. He was living proof that the message of Peter and John was valid.

Without a doubt, one of the strongest arguments for the Christian faith is a transformed life. The greatest commentary of Jesus' love and power is written in the words and actions of His people. You are a living biography of Jesus, perhaps the only "book" about Him some people will ever read. They may not read the gospel literature you leave for them on the restaurant counter. They may not listen to the cassette tape you give them which explains the gospel message. They may not even read the beautiful Bible you give them. But they will look at your life. Like it or not, people are going to determine what they think about God by observing the way you live. That's why we need to be a witness as much as we articulate our witness.

As soon as people hear that you are a Christian, they will start watching you carefully. In some ways they just want to see you slip up so they can have something to hang their doubts on. But when you live the life instead of just talk the talk, your life will be a powerful testimony that at least forces unbelievers to acknowledge that what you believe is real to you. And once they realize it is real in your life, they might start to consider how it could be real in theirs as well.

Preparing for Divine Appointments

Wouldn't it be nice if in your daily planner you could have a spot for "Divine Appointments" just to be sure you didn't miss any? Is there a way we can know? To answer that I'd like to focus on two vital questions Paul asked the Lord on the Damascus Road on the day of his conversion: "Who are You, Lord?" and "What do You want me to do?" (Acts 9:5,6). These two significant questions launched the great apostle into a lifetime ministry that changed the world of the first century. Keeping these two questions in mind each day will help you prepare to welcome divine appointments when God inserts them into your daily routine.

For all practical purposes, we'll spend the rest of our lives seeking the answer to the first question: "Who are You, Lord?" But what better way to spend your life than getting to know the One who created you? After all, you were made to know God and have fellowship with Him.

Philippians 3:10 tells us that Paul's determined purpose in life was to know Christ. A literal translation of that verse might run, "To become more progressively and intimately acquainted with Him."

Does this goal describe you? Is your daily purpose in life to know God? If so, then you are in a perfect position to recognize His divine appointments for sharing His love with those you meet day by day. The better you know Him, the more you will see people the way He sees them and recognize the opportunities for doing good He places in your path.

The second question we need to ask God daily is, "What do You want me to do?" Many Christians live in turmoil, unable to impact their world for Christ, because they never ask God, "What do You want me to do today?" They just get up in the morning and go their own way instead of seeking out God's plan for them.

I know this has become somewhat of a cliché, but it's still true: God loves you and has a wonderful plan for your life, a unique, custom-designed plan just for you. He doesn't lay out a detailed blueprint of your whole life all at once. He reveals His plan one step at a time. Year by year, ask, "Lord, what do You want me to do this year?" Month by month, ask, "Lord, what do You want me to do this month?" Day by day, ask, "Lord, what do You want me to do today? Make Your will known to me!"

Nothing is more exciting than knowing you're in the midst of a divine appointment and that God is using you at that moment for His purposes.

CHAPTER EIGHT

$\mathcal{G}$IVING AWAY THE GOOD NEWS

JESUS MAKES IT OBVIOUS that the good news of salvation which has set our hearts ablaze is not just for us but for everyone. Jesus commands us, "Go into all the world and preach the gospel to every creature" (Mark 16:15). The gospel isn't a treasure to be hoarded; it's a gift to be shared. When we talk about spreading the passion within us to touch others and impact our world for God, we must talk about communicating the gospel.

But what is the gospel? It's a word we often hear thrown about, but what exactly does it mean? A literal definition of the word is "good news." Before we can preach this good news we need to have a working knowledge of what the gospel is and what it is not. Understanding what this good news is will help us better appreciate the scope and power of the gospel message we are to spread.

What the Gospel Is Not

It's not hard to find many distortions of the gospel. Some people preach what we might call the *easy believism gospel*. This distortion teaches us to "just ask Jesus Christ into your life, and He'll be your best friend and give you peace, joy, love, and fulfillment, and everything will be great." Now, essentially that's true. The gospel promises all that and much more. But the easy believism gospel fails to mention the penalty of rejecting Christ and the difference in one's lifestyle that must follow conversion. It implies that you can receive Christ and go to heaven when you die but continue to live the way you want to on earth. Easy believism speaks of heaven but not hell, forgiveness but not repentance, happiness but not holiness. It's simply a watered-down version of the real gospel.

Another distortion of the gospel might be called the *legalistic gospel*. People who promote this variation say that unless we preach rules and regulations, we have not fully preached the gospel. In other words, they say you must obey certain rules to be saved, such as be baptized or belong to a certain denomination. While those of the easy believism persuasion attempt to take away from the gospel, those from the legalistic perspective try to add to it. That doesn't sound like terribly good news to me.

What the Gospel Is

In contrast to these popular misconceptions, the gospel is essentially this: God loves human beings, but they have broken His laws, fallen miserably short of His glory, and sinned against Him. As a result of our sin and rebellion, we have an emptiness, loneliness, and void in our lives. Not only do we face the temporal consequences of our sin, but we face the future consequences as well, specifically judgment and hell.

Knowing our hopeless situation, God took drastic measures by sending His Son Jesus to earth to die on a cross in our place and take the judgment we deserved upon Himself. Consequently, we must respond to Jesus Christ and His message. We must believe in Him and receive Him into our lives as our Lord and Savior. In doing so we must repent, which means to turn away from sin and turn toward God. If we fail to repent, we have not fully responded to the gospel.

This is only a thumbnail sketch of the gospel, of course. Later in the chapter we will expand on this definition by considering three specific steps to salvation. Understanding these three steps will help prepare you to share the gospel with people who need it so desperately. But first we're going to look at an example of how the gospel was presented in the first-century church.

A Golden Opportunity

Acts 26 describes how Paul shared the gospel with the Jewish king, Herod Agrippa II. Paul's message in this chapter gives us the gospel in a nutshell. I hope it will also inspire us, as Paul's bold presentation prompted this powerful, ungodly man to say, "You almost persuade me to become a Christian" (v. 28).

Agrippa was the last in the wicked line of Herods we read about in the New Testament. His great-grandfather slaughtered all the male children in Bethlehem two years old and under because of his paranoia about the birth of the Messiah (Matthew 2:16-18). Agrippa's grandfather murdered John the Baptist (Matthew 14:6-10). Several years later, Agrippa's father, Agrippa I, executed the apostle James and arrested Peter (Acts 12:1-4). In Acts 26 we find Herod Agrippa II facing the foremost follower of the Man and movement his great-grandfather, grandfather, and father tried to eradicate.

This passage gives an interesting study in contrasts. On one hand we have Agrippa and the elite of Rome in all their splendor and glory, sitting regally upon their thrones. On the other hand we have the apostle Paul, brought before them in chains. Yet Paul possessed something of infinite value and wasn't afraid to share it: The peace of Christ in his heart.

Paul's presentation of the gospel in Acts 26:4-29 includes his personal testimony, a brief but pointed outline of what it means to become a Christian, and a specific appeal to Agrippa to believe. In it we find vital principles for effectively sharing our faith.

The Power of a Changed Life

Paul begins by describing what he was before he met Christ and how God dramatically turned around his life (vv. 4-23). In these verses he demonstrates one of the most effective tools you and I have in our spiritual toolbox for sharing the gospel: Our personal testimony. This is *your* good news, the account or story of how you personally came to know Jesus Christ. It is one of the most potent resources you can draw from because it is uniquely your story. Though it is vital to know the Scriptures and be able to give a defense of your faith, there is enormous power in the simple story of how you personally came to be changed by Jesus Christ.

Too often we allow our personal testimonies to become clouded with religious jargon we might call "Christianese." We interject phrases and clichés that only a Christian would understand, like, "Yes, when I was saved, redeemed, washed in the blood, and the Holy Ghost came into my life, I was set on fire for God. Now I'm a sanctified vessel for the Lord, and I am involved in evangelism and discipleship."

I don't mean to denigrate any of these terms, for indeed they are biblical. The question is, will unbelievers understand what on earth you're talking about? They may be perplexed when you say that a "ghost" came into you, even if it is holy! And what does it mean when you say you are "on fire" for God? What do the words "discipleship" and "evangelism" mean to non-Christians? Many times we assume people know what we're talking about, but to them we're speaking a foreign language. In doing so we miss the point of the personal testimony.

Your personal testimony is a tool for bridging the gap between yourself and the person you're speaking to. As a Christian you've had the unique advantage of being on both sides of that gap. You remember how it was without the Lord and you know what it's like to walk with Him now. By describing where you once were and by communicating what Jesus has done for you, you give hope that the same thing can happen to him or her.

What's nice about sharing your own experience with Jesus is that it's personal and human. Instead of preaching, "*Your* life is all messed up, and *you* need to change *your* ways," you're saying, "Let *me* tell you how messed up *my* life was and what Jesus did for *me*." You're not only taking some of the pressure off the listener, you're also helping him realize that you weren't born a Christian; you changed. Your testimony subtly encourages your friend to consider a change also.

Many unbelievers think that all Christians have flipped their lids. They don't realize that many of these "fanatics" have come from the very circumstances in which they find themselves—or even worse. Sometimes I meet Christians who seem to glow and radiate with God's love and am shocked to find that they have come out of the drug scene or worked the streets as prostitutes. I couldn't have guessed the dramatic work of God's Spirit in their lives.

Your testimony is a tool to show someone what a difference Jesus has made in your life and what He can do in the lives of others. We often forget that Paul used to be Saul. Still, he was able to put his sinful past behind him. That should give us hope as well, and give hope to all who hear our personal testimony.

Once we build the bridge of our personal testimony, the stage is set to share the message of the gospel.

The Gospel in a Nutshell

Immediately following his testimony, Paul got down to brass tacks with Agrippa. He laid out the gospel in a nutshell, giving one of the clearest definitions of conversion found in all of Scripture. Mark it in your Bible and in your mind. This is one text you will want to commit to memory. In Acts 26:18, Paul defines conversion in terms of what God called him to do in his ministry: "To open their eyes and to turn them from darkness to light, and from the power of Satan to God, that they may receive forgiveness of sins and an inheritance among those who are sanctified by faith in Me."

This verse contains three important steps leading to salvation and two steps that follow it. This is the process of conversion. An accurate presentation of the gospel contains all these elements.

1. His eyes must be opened by the Holy Spirit.
2. He must turn from darkness to light.
3. He must turn from the power of Satan to God.
4. He will receive the forgiveness of sins.
5. He will receive an inheritance.

Let's look at each of these elements one by one.

Step 1: Eyes must be opened. Before unbelievers can be converted, their eyes must be opened. If their eyes are not opened, they can't take any of the steps that follow.

The Bible teaches that we are all spiritually blind prior to conversion: "If our gospel is veiled, it is veiled to those who are perishing, whose minds the god of this age [the devil] has blinded, who do not believe, lest the light of the gospel of the glory of Christ, who is the image of God, should shine on them" (2 Corinthians 4:3,4).

Some people don't understand why they should become Christians. You can give them clever analogies and insightful illustrations, but you might as well be talking to a wall because it doesn't penetrate. Satan has blinded their eyes and they won't be converted until their eyes are opened.

It is the work of the Holy Spirit to heal spiritual blindness and allow unbelievers to see the "light of the gospel of the glory of Christ." The only thing we can do to make it happen is pray. Prayer is vital to the ministry of sharing the gospel. We must pray for those to whom we witness that God will open their blind eyes so they can see the steps they must take to be saved.

Step 2: Turn from darkness to light. Once unbelievers' eyes are opened and they see their need for Jesus Christ, they must turn from the darkness of their old life to the light of new life in Christ. Darkness and light symbolize the two different kingdoms and lifestyles in the Bible. Darkness represents living in rebellion against God, seeking our own satisfaction and pleasures, and going the way of the world. Light represents living in obedience to God. To live in the light means that we are walking according to God's ways and purposes.

Interestingly, a person can have his eyes opened to his spiritual need and still not turn from darkness to light. I have met people who say, "I know what you are saying to me is true. I know I need to give my life to Jesus Christ. I know He died on the cross for me and rose from the dead. I know that I'm a sinner and that if I died right now I would go to hell. But I'm just not ready to receive Christ." Their eyes are open, but they haven't turned from darkness to light. At this point, they are not saved.

Still others delude themselves by saying, "I'm going to heaven because my eyes are opened. I realize Jesus is the Son of God, and I believe He is the Lord. Therefore, I'm saved." This person is getting close, but he still must take the next step of turning from darkness to light.

This leads to an important point about the gospel message. There are some tasks only God can do and some only we can do. Only God can save, but only unbelievers can repent. God can't repent for us; He gave us a free will and the ability to say yes or no to Him.

Turning from darkness to light is the point where unbelievers whose eyes have been opened say, "This is it, Lord. I'm coming to You now." Then they must also take the next step of turning from Satan's control to God's control.

Step 3: Turn from Satan's power to God. People who don't know Jesus Christ are under the control of the devil. They have been "taken captive to do his will" (2 Timothy 2:26). One of the greatest deceptions the devil has ever pulled off is causing people to question his existence. Meanwhile he manipulates and controls them.

Unbelievers are living hostages of the devil. They have existed under his influence and direction their whole life. Many have even knowingly pledged their allegiance to him. To be saved, one's loyalty and devotion must be promised to God.

Step 4: Forgiveness of sins. Once the unbeliever has taken the first three steps of having his eyes opened and then turning from darkness to light and from Satan to God, he enjoys the wonderful privilege of forgiveness. Everybody wants to be forgiven because everybody carries around guilt. Guilt is the result of sin. The reason your non-Christian friends *feel* guilt is because they *are* guilty of sinning against God.

People are desperate to find solutions to their guilt. Thousands of dollars are spent on psychologists who will try to explain away guilt. But it's still there. Other people try to drown their guilt, to numb its effect with drinking, drugs, sensual pleasures, or even religious ritual. But guilt remains. The exasperating truth about guilt is that it can intensify years after the sin has been committed, and the individual may reap the results of that sin 10, 20, or 30 years later. The Bible warns, "Be sure your sin will find you out" (Numbers 32:23) and "Do not be deceived, God is not mocked; for whatever a man sows, that will he also reap" (Galatians 6:7).

The good news that unbelievers need to hear is that God can take away all their sins, wiping their slate clean. David wrote, "As far as the east is from the west, so far has He removed our transgressions from us" (Psalm 103:12). What must unbelievers do to receive His forgiveness? Their eyes must be opened so they can see their need for God. They need to repent, to turn from darkness to light and from the power of Satan to God. If they do this they will receive forgiveness of sin.

Many people today think they are forgiven when they really are not. They misunderstand the message of forgiveness in passages like 1 John 1:9: "If we confess our sins, He is faithful and just to forgive us our sin and to cleanse us from all unrighteousness." They pray something like, "Yes, I have sinned. I confess it in Jesus' name. Amen." Then they go out and do it again. They repeat this routine over and over.

These people neglect the condition of the promise in 1 John 1:9. Confession means more than simply admitting your sin. The word "confess" in the original Greek means "to agree with." In this case, we agree with God to look at sin the same way He looks at it. God hates sin. Therefore, if I am in agreement with Him I will hate it as He does. I will be genuinely sorry about my sin and I will want to turn away from it. That is true confession.

What would you think if someone came up to you, smacked you across the face, and then quickly said, "I'm sorry. I don't know what came over me. I can't believe I just did that. You are my best friend. Please forgive me."

With your face still throbbing you might say, "Boy, that really hurt, but I forgive you."

Then, *whack!* he does it again! "I'm sorry," he says. "I'll never do it again. Believe me, I mean it this time."

And you once more reply, "Okay, I forgive you."

Then, *smack!* he does it even harder. Suddenly his plea for forgiveness has a hollow ring to it. The words are meaningless.

In essence, we do the same thing when we ask God for forgiveness one minute and then go out and deliberately sin again the next. We're not truly sorry for our sin. We may be sorry about getting caught and about the consequences of our sin, but that's not true repentance. The Bible says, "Godly sorrow produces repentance" (2 Corinthians 7:10). We need to be sorry to the point that we don't want to do it again.

Don't lead new believers to think that they won't sin again after receiving God's forgiveness. We're all human, and the Bible clearly makes allowance for our sin. Scripture tells us that when we sin "we have an Advocate with the Father, Jesus Christ the righteous" (1 John 2:1). Nevertheless, we must help new Christians realize there is a difference between sinning and truly being sorry for it, versus asking God to forgive us and continuing to live in a pattern of sin.

Step 5: Receiving an inheritance. Finally, when all the steps above have been taken, new believers can be assured that God will grant them "an inheritance among those who are sanctified by faith in [Christ]" (Acts 26:18). They now have the hope of heaven as well as the joy of knowing that Jesus will personally come back for them as a groom comes for his bride. As a child of God, they will enjoy the privileges of any child whose father is powerful and wealthy. In this case, our Father is all-powerful and just happens to own everything! What an inheritance!

The Moment of Decision

Paul could have stopped his presentation before Agrippa at this point and said, "Thank you very much, God bless all of you, I'll be praying for you," and walked out of the court. But Paul wasn't finished. He says in Acts 26:27, "King Agrippa, do you believe the prophets? I know that you do believe." That's a pretty bold thing for a man in chains to say to a king! It could have cost Paul his life. But he was giving Agrippa an opportunity to believe, as indicated by Agrippa's response in verse 28: "You almost persuade me to become a Christian."

Exactly what Agrippa meant by that statement is hard to say. Was he making light of Paul's attempt to convert him? "Are you actually trying to convert *me*, the king?" Or was his interest genuine? "You know, you're making a lot of sense here, Paul, and I find myself being persuaded!"

I don't know. But whatever the case, Paul's intentions were clear. He stood uncompromisingly for the truth of the gospel in giving Agrippa an opportunity to believe.

How often do we share the gospel and bring someone right to the brink of believing, then say, "So, just think about it. I'll pray for you"? Instead, we should ask that person, "Do you believe? Would you like to accept Jesus Christ right now? I'd love to pray with you."

I think the reason many of us have not led more people to the Lord is because we have not invited them to believe. It's like going on a fishing trip and having your tackle box out and all your lures ready, then dropping your line in the water with one small omission: no hook! Then you go home and say, "I can't understand why I never catch any fish."

Many of us "fish" that way in personal evangelism. We never put hooks on our lines. Or, to use another fishing analogy, we don't throw out the net. "Well, let the fish jump into the boat. The net's here. Can't they see it from down there?" We need to throw out the net and see what happens.

"But what if they say no?" you may ask. So they say no. I think we are more afraid that they will say yes. What do we do then? Then we have the privilege of leading someone from darkness to light and from the power of Satan to God so that they may receive the forgiveness of sins and an inheritance among those who are sanctified. It is one of the greatest joys we will ever know next to our own personal salvation.

I pray that we would have the kind of boldness Paul had and not be intimidated by someone's position, wealth, success, or whatever else would daunt us from sharing our faith. And may we, like Paul, give people an opportunity to respond. (I have dealt with the subject of leading others to Christ and discipling them more thoroughly in my book *Giving God Your Best—Studies in Discipleship.*)

The Whole Truth

We must be sure to present the whole gospel to the unbelievers we meet. We need to tell them the whole truth and nothing but the truth, so help us God. We must tell them the good news that God loves them and that He will forgive them and give them peace, joy, and hope. But we must also let them know the penalty that awaits them if they reject Jesus Christ. If we do not tell them that, we are not being completely honest.

If they reject Jesus by claiming that they are happy with their life and they don't have any great need at the moment, we are failing to tell them the most important truth about the Christian life. A certain judgment awaits them if they reject this loving offer of forgiveness. The Scripture asks, "How shall we escape if we neglect so great a salvation?" (Hebrews 2:3). We have eternal life and are going to heaven. A lot of us pussyfoot around that fact. We don't want to say it. We're afraid it will turn people away from Christ. But it might be the very thing that turns them toward Him and brings them to their senses.

Don't be ashamed of this message. Express it in love, but say it and leave the results up to the Holy Spirit. Paul wrote, "I am not ashamed of the gospel of Christ, for it is the power of God to salvation" (Romans 1:16). May God help us by the power of His Holy Spirit not to be ashamed of this gospel in a time when it is so desperately needed.

It seems to me that in these last days the devil is dramatically stepping up his efforts to keep us from sharing the gospel. I see people all around standing up for the most perverse and ungodly causes and lies. Isn't it time for us as believers to stand up for the truth and proclaim the gospel? Why don't you ask the Lord right now to give you a refill of His power so you will be outspoken for the gospel? As the first-century believers prayed on one occasion, "Grant to Your servants that with all boldness they may speak Your word" (Acts 4:29). I'm sure God will honor a prayer like that. He certainly did many years ago, and He will again today.

CHAPTER NINE

LEADING OTHERS TO CHRIST

HOW OFTEN DO YOU SHARE the good news of the gospel with others? It's one thing to understand what the gospel is and know the biblical steps that result in unbelievers being converted. It's quite another to be committed to the ongoing ministry of sharing your faith and leading others to Christ. Yet this is a commitment Jesus calls on-fire believers to make.

Christianity Today polled its readers to determine why believers are so reluctant to share their faith. The poll revealed that an impressive 87 percent of the respondents agreed that every Christian is responsible for evangelism. But only 52 percent have been more active in telling others about Christ in the past year than ever before.

Why weren't they sharing their faith? Forty-three percent said they were too timid; 40 percent feared how people would respond; and a surprising 49 percent—nearly half—claimed they weren't able to do evangelism as well as the professionals (pastors, missionaries, evangelists, etc.).

If you are reluctant to evangelize, do you identify with any of these obstacles? In this chapter we will meet a layman from the early church who was on fire for God and mightily used by Him in this high privilege of personally leading others to Jesus Christ. The principles for evangelism he exemplifies will equip you to step out and share the gospel with those around you who so desperately need it.

Ready to Reach Out

Philip wasn't one of the apostles like Peter or John. He was just an ordinary believer who was full of the Holy Spirit and wisdom. Like Stephen, Philip had distinguished himself with his passion for serving Christ and was appointed to minister to the physical needs of church members while the apostles focused on preaching and prayer (Acts 6:1-6).

Yet Philip also made himself available to God for reaching the lost. In Acts 8 we find him involved in two forms of evangelism. In verses 4-8 we read that Philip was used by God in what we would call *mass* evangelism. He went down to Samaria, an area populated by those who were "rejects" to the Jews, and preached Christ to great crowds. God through him performed miracles of healing and spiritual deliverance and many people believed. Philip was instrumental in effecting a great spiritual awakening in the area.

Then God directed Philip to shift gears and leave the work in Samaria to minister to a single individual who needed Christ: the Ethiopian eunuch (vv. 26-40). We call this *personal* evangelism.

We never know when we get up in the morning what God has in store for us. He may want us to address a group. They might be friends, family, fellow students, or coworkers. Then again He may have just one person in mind. He may lead you to an individual sitting alone on a park bench or to someone pumping gas for you. It might be a homeless person huddled in a doorway or a person sitting in a Rolls Royce.

When we think of evangelism, we often think of reaching the down-and-out, like those on the streets with no place to call home. Yes, they need the gospel. But there are also people who are up-and-out. They may have everything this world has to offer and still be empty and searching. That was the situation with the foreign dignitary Philip met on the road to Gaza. Apparently this man had all the world could offer, but he was still missing something in life.

We can sometimes be misled by appearances and assume that certain people would never be interested in hearing about Jesus Christ. But as Philip's encounter with the Samaritans and the Ethiopian eunuch illustrates, that assumption is invalid. God can use us anytime and anywhere to share the gospel with any group or person at any social, economic, or spiritual level.

Four Principles for Effective Evangelism

So how can we become effective in sharing our faith? How can we make evangelism a lifestyle as the early believers did? Let's examine the account of Philip's meeting with the Ethiopian eunuch and discover four important principles for leading others to Jesus Christ.

1. You need a burden for the lost. Effective evangelism doesn't begin with a program; it begins with a burden. That's obviously what moved Philip to journey into Samaria to reach out to a class of people regarded by the Jews as inferior. He had no human reason to cross that social barrier.

His burden also prepared him for ministering to the Ethiopian eunuch, a man of much higher social standing than himself. Instead of thinking, "This man has it all together. He wouldn't want to hear about the gospel from someone like me," Philip was ready to obey the Holy Spirit directing him to go one-on-one with a very important but very needy foreign official.

We hear so much about the need to evangelize. We have programs to mobilize the church to be actively involved in evangelism. We have classes teaching us how to defend the faith. Still, many believers are reluctant to share their faith. I believe it's often because we lack a genuine, God-given burden for the lost. If we don't have a real concern for unbelievers, all the principles and programs we put together are useless. Our witnessing must be motivated by a compelling compassion for those we are trying to reach.

We must really care about those who are without Christ. People can tell if we are genuinely interested in them. Some Christians share their faith only out of a sense of duty, thinking God or their pastor expect it of them. They pretend to be interested in others only to coax them into a decision for Christ. Unbelievers can see through such a facade.

We must have the same compassion Jesus had for the lost. In Luke 13:34, Jesus' compassion and burden for His people is revealed when He says, "O Jerusalem, Jerusalem, the one who kills the prophets and stones those who are sent to her! How often I wanted to gather your children together, as a hen gathers her brood under her wings, but you were not willing!" And we read that He wept over the city (Luke 19:41).

You might say, "That was Jesus. He was God. I'm just a human being. How can I be expected to have a burden for the lost like His?" Yet Philippians 2:5 tells us, "Let this mind be in you which was also in Christ Jesus." Our daily growth in Christ's likeness should include an increased burden for the lost.

Paul echoed the same burden in Romans 9:2,3: "I have great sorrow and continual grief in my heart. For I could wish that I myself were accursed from Christ for my brethren, my kinsmen according to the flesh." Paul was saying, "I would give up my salvation if that would make it possible for my fellow Jews to come to faith in Christ." What an amazing statement! Who of us would wish ourselves a place in hell so that unbelievers might have a place in heaven? With a burden like that, no wonder Paul had such a powerful and effective ministry of evangelism.

Alexander MacLaren once said, "You tell me the depth of a Christian's compassion, and I will tell you the measure of his usefulness." How deep is your compassion? Do you believe a person outside of Jesus Christ is going to face a terrifying judgment? If so, why aren't you doing something about it? It may be because you lack the motivation of a burden.

You can't get compassion for the lost by going to a class or by reading a manual. You only get compassion by going to God in prayer. Pray that God will give you His burden, His vision, and His passion for those who are outside the faith. Without that, nothing else about evangelism really matters.

Your prayers for burden and compassion may be encouraged by knowing four things that are true of every unbeliever. These needs are more fully examined in Billy Graham's book *The Work of an Evangelist*.

First, *there is an essential emptiness in every life without Jesus Christ*. No matter how much money a person has, how much power he possesses, how well-known he is, or how nice a car he owns, there's a hollowness and spiritual void in his life. Not long ago I read an article about an actress who at one time was one of the most popular performers in Hollywood. She said a lot of actors feel a kind of hole in their hearts, an unfocused ache they try to fix by eating too much, taking drugs, or getting involved in illicit sex.

We assume that the rich and famous of the world have everything they need and could care less about the gospel. Yet who's surprised anymore when a Hollywood celebrity overdoses on drugs, ends up at a substance abuse clinic, submits to psychotherapy, or commits suicide? A noted Hollywood actor said, "I found that I couldn't shove enough drugs, women, cars, stereos, houses, and stardom in there to make me feel good. I guess that's why a lot of people overdose. They get to the point where the hole is so big they die."

The rich and famous have everything this world has to offer, but they have found how empty it really is. It's the emptiness every unbeliever knows. They are waiting for someone to bring them the good news.

Second, *there is a loneliness in every individual*. No matter how many friends people have, they still feel this deep-seated loneliness. They may be at a party or in a crowded mall when this sense of loneliness sweeps over them. It's the same for everyone. When you get down to it, it's really a loneliness for the God who created and loves them.

Third, *all people live with a sense of guilt*. Billy Graham says, "This is perhaps the most universal of all human experiences, and it is devastating. The head of a mental institution in London said, 'I could release half of my patients if I could but find a way to rid them of their sense of guilt.'"

We Christians know that guilt is a symptom of an even deeper problem called sin. People feel guilt because they are guilty! Only Jesus Christ can get to the root of the problem and forgive them of their sins.

Fourth, *there is a universal fear of death*. People may not acknowledge it. They may laugh at death when you speak to them about it. But everyone fears it as well as what may happen after they die.

These four universal needs abide in the souls of all humans. Remember when you had no assurance of life after death? Remember when God was alien to you? How about the burden of guilt you used to bear and the happy relief when that weight was lifted by the mercy of God? How can we not live with compassion for the lost? If reaching unbelievers with the truth of Jesus' love is a burden, may it be a load that we joyfully accept as passionate believers.

C.H. Spurgeon, speaking of the need for Christians to be burdened for the lost, said, "The Holy Spirit will move [the lost] by first moving you. If you can rest without their being saved, they will rest too. But if you are filled with an agony for them, if you cannot bear that they should be lost, you will soon find that they are uneasy too. I hope you will get into such a state that you will dream about your child or your hearer perishing for lack of Christ, and start up at once and begin to cry, 'O God, give me converts, or I die.' Then you will have converts." That's the daily prayer that builds a burden within us: "O God, give me converts, or I die."

2. You must be led by the Holy Spirit. After being directed by God to go to a location on the road from Jerusalem to Gaza, Philip saw the Ethiopian eunuch sitting in his chariot reading from the scrolls of the prophet Isaiah. "Then the Spirit said to Philip, 'Go near and overtake this chariot'" (Acts 8:29). Philip's interaction with this unbeliever was the result of being led by the Holy Spirit.

Should we expect to be led by the Holy Spirit in our attempts at evangelism? Definitely. Does God lead us to people by an audible voice? Not generally. I've found that the Lord often leads me by impression. I'm not talking about some mystical feeling that comes over me. I just sense that I should do something. For example, I might see a person in a crowded room and suddenly have a desire to go and speak to him. I often don't even know what my first words will be. God doesn't give me a detailed blueprint of what He has in mind. I just sense the leading of the Holy Spirit and I follow it.

God generally leads us one step at a time. If we obey Him when He directs us to go speak to someone, He will give us what to say when we need it. If we don't take the first step, we shouldn't expect further direction. The best way to prepare for the Spirit's leading each day is to tell God when you wake up that you're ready to follow Him. You might pray a prayer similar to Isaiah's: "Here am I! Send me" (Isaiah 6:8). Only yours may sound more like, "I'm ready to share the gospel wherever You lead me today. If it's to one person or a group of people, I'm available. Please call on me." If you pray a prayer like that, you may be surprised to find how quickly God will utilize your services!

I remember praying like that many years ago. I had only been a believer a few weeks. One day I decided to go down to the beach in Newport Beach, California, for a baptismal service sponsored by Calvary Chapel. When I arrived, instead of seeing the hundreds of people who normally attend the baptisms, I found the beach largely deserted. I soon learned that I had arrived too late. The baptism had already taken place.

I thought, *I can't believe I missed the baptism. Why did this happen? I wanted to be there so badly.*

Then I overheard a small group of Christians sitting nearby on the beach singing praise songs, so I walked over and joined them. The group didn't seem to have a leader. They were just singing together.

As I sat there I sensed I should share something I had recently read in the Bible. I wasn't a pastor or a teacher. But I followed God's leading and spoke up. "Excuse me, could I just say a couple of words right now?"

Every eye was on me. My mouth went dry and my voice quivered when I spoke. My little talk lasted all of five minutes, and I was greatly relieved when it was over.

"Oh Lord, that was so great!" I prayed silently. "Thank You for using me. I can't wait to tell my friends how You opened up this opportunity today."

But the Holy Spirit was just getting started. While I had been speaking, a couple of girls joined the little meeting and they assumed I was the leader. After I was done, they came over and said, "Pastor, we missed the baptism. Would you baptize us?"

"I can't do that," I quietly explained. "I'm not a minister. I don't even know how to baptize someone. No, I'm sorry. I just can't."

Then I sensed the Lord saying, "Do it." My desire to obey God was greater than my fear, so I told the girls I would baptize them. I said to the group, "These girls want to be baptized. Let's go down to the cove." I stood up and started walking down to the cove with about 30 people following me. I thought, *What have I gotten myself into? This is crazy!*

Finally we came to the area where the baptisms were usually held. As I was getting ready to baptize these girls, a crowd of people began to gather. Again I felt an impression from God's Spirit, this time saying, "Preach."

I was terrified, but having already taken the previous steps with Him, I thought, *Why not?* So I started to speak to the crowd. Some of them even came forward to receive Jesus Christ. I led them in prayer and had the privilege of baptizing five people that day.

It's a good thing God didn't show me that morning everything He had in mind for the rest of the day. I probably wouldn't have gone to the beach. But that's often how the Lord leads us in our evangelistic endeavors—one step at a time. If you will remain open and available to His leading, and then obey Him step-by-step, you'll be amazed at what He can accomplish through you.

3. Being obedient. The third quality we find in Philip's life that caused him to effectively lead others to Jesus Christ was his obedience to God. It's not enough merely to know what God wants you to do; you must respond to it. And Philip did just that when the Lord directed him to go down to a desert area on the road from Jerusalem to Gaza.

Philip easily could have argued with the Lord. "What? Leave Samaria? Lord, have You noticed how many people are coming to faith here? Have You seen the miracles? Now You want me to travel 80 miles to the desert? For what? Why don't You call someone from Jerusalem to do it? That's 30 miles closer. Get one of the apostles. Maybe John or Andrew."

Of course, Philip said no such thing. In fact, the Bible doesn't record a single word of protest coming from Philip's lips. We see simple obedience. I'm sure that's precisely why God called him. I suppose there were many great instruments God could have used that day to reach this important person from a distant kingdom, but He chose to use an ordinary man. Philip was open, available, and obedient, so God used him. If you make yourself the same, He will use you as well.

4. You need to know Scripture. Philip wasn't only obedient, he was prepared. Philip knew God's Word and was equipped to share the gospel.

It's amazing to see how God orchestrates situations for the gospel to be shared. I call them "divine setups." That's when you run into a person who is at a point in life where he is ready to believe. At the same time, God has been working in your life, preparing you for this encounter. Maybe you have just read a portion of Scripture that answers some of the questions that person will ask. It's so exciting to realize you are in the perfect will of God. But to be in this position you must be prepared.

The official from Ethiopia had come to Jerusalem searching for God. I'm sure this V.I.P. created quite a stir when his retinue entered the city that day. The officials in Jerusalem probably rolled out the red carpet to such a man, showing him the glories of this famous city known to be one of the religious capitals of the world.

Although he came to meet God in Jerusalem, all he found was a cold, lifeless religion. The Ethiopian dignitary no doubt left disillusioned because he didn't find what he was looking for. He did leave with one valuable treasure, however: a copy of the Scriptures. We're not told if he had all of the Old Testament or only Isaiah's scroll. As Philip approached him, the Ethiopian was reading Isaiah 53:7,8, prophetic words about the sacrifice of Jesus. He was at the right place at the right time reading the right Scripture when God brought Philip into his life.

Philip asked, "Do you understand what you are reading?" (Acts 8:30).

"How can I unless someone guides me? . . . Of whom does the prophet say this, of himself or of some other man?" (vv. 31,34).

What if Philip had been ignorant of Scripture? He might have said, "That's a great question. Can I get back to you on this? What's your fax number?" But Philip knew the Word "and beginning at this Scripture, preached Jesus to him" (v. 35).

Stop and think for a moment: When you came to faith in Jesus Christ, did it take a five-point sermon to get to you? Probably not. It might have been one simple sentence based on Scripture. In my case, one statement struck my heart like a lightning bolt from heaven. The speaker that day stated, "Jesus said you're either for Me or against Me."

I don't know what else the preacher said, but I did hear that snippet from Scripture, and it stuck with me.

You don't need to know the Bible backward and forward to be able to bring someone to Jesus. But the more of God's Word you know, the better prepared you will be to respond to the questions people ask.

You might think, *But what if they don't believe the Bible is the Word of God?* Use it anyway. God's Word is "sharper than any two-edged sword" and can penetrate any shield. They may say they don't believe the Bible, but it's still His Word and still effectual whether they believe it's His Word or not.

Let me illustrate. Suppose I'm on a battlefield with my sword drawn, approaching my adversary. Suddenly he says, "I don't believe your sword is sharp. In fact, I don't even believe your sword exists. It's simply an illusion!"

How can I convince such a person of both the reality and effectiveness of my sword? Should I tell him what kind of steel it's made of, or perhaps describe my past successes with it? I think the best tactic would be to use it on him! Thrust him through, and then he'll know exactly how sharp it is! The same is true of the Word of God, which Ephesians 6:17 compares to a sword, an essential weapon for the spiritual soldier.

In Isaiah 55:10,11, God says, "As the rain comes down, and the snow from heaven, and do not return there, but water the earth, and make it bring forth and bud, that it may give seed to the sower and bread to the eater, so shall My word be that goes forth from My mouth; it shall not return to Me void, but it shall accomplish what I please, and it shall prosper in the thing for which I sent it."

My words and your words may accomplish nothing. But God's Word always accomplishes that for which God intends it. For that reason, learn it. Memorize it. Know it. As you speak God's Word, it will penetrate, even as it did with the Ethiopian who believed and was baptized (Acts 8:36-38).

God's Word is our primary weapon in evangelism. It is not designed to destroy life, but to give it. It is not to be used to harm but, like a surgeon's scalpel, to save. Just as a builder knows his tools and an artist knows his brushes and pens, we need to know the Bible. As Paul said to Timothy, "Be diligent to present yourself approved to God, a worker who does not need to be ashamed, rightly dividing the word of truth" (2 Timothy 2:15).

First Peter 3:15 says, "But sanctify the Lord God in your hearts, and always be ready to give a defense to everyone who asks you a reason for the hope that is in you, with meekness and fear." That phrase "give an answer . . . to everyone who asks you" comes from the Greek word *apologia* from which we get our English word "apologetic." It means a legal defense as in a court of law. Always be ready to give a reasoned defense for what you believe. Know what you believe, and be ready to share it.

Why Me?

We might ask, "Why does God even use us in the ministry of evangelism? No doubt He could do His work far more efficiently without us." While it may be fair to ask the question, it is irrelevant. God has chosen to communicate His message through people.

It is worth noting that no person in the New Testament came to faith apart from the agency of a human being. Think about Cornelius in Acts 10, the spiritually seeking Roman centurion to whom an angel actually appeared. It seems logical that the angelic messenger would have proclaimed the gospel to this man right then and there. Instead, the angel directed Cornelius to Peter, whom the Holy Spirit had prepared in advance for the meeting. Peter shared the gospel with the soldier and his family and they were converted.

You may say, "I just thought of someone who came to Christ without a person being utilized: Saul of Tarsus. After all, wasn't he converted on the road to Damascus by Jesus Himself?" True, but you must consider that Saul's heart had already been prepared through the dramatic impact of the life and death of Stephen, as described in Acts 7. I have no question that Stephen's fearless and courageous testimony before the self-righteous Saul caused his hardened heart to soften, preparing the way for his conversion. And after Saul's encounter with Jesus on the road, God used another person in Saul's conversion experience: Ananias, who sought Paul out and prayed for him.

God doesn't *need* us to reach a spiritually dying world, but He clearly *wants* us. When we fail to obey His command to make disciples, we not only flagrantly disobey Him but miss out on one of the greatest of all His blessings: the privilege of joining with Him to reach the people for whom He died.

In Romans 10:14 Paul asks the question, "How then shall they call on Him in whom they have not believed? And how shall they believe in Him of whom they have not heard? And how shall they hear without a preacher?" In the original Greek, the phrase "without a preacher" could also be translated "without one preaching." The Phillip's translation says, "How can they hear unless someone proclaims Him?"

The emphasis is not on a preacher *per se*, but on preaching. This refutes the idea that we're dependent on so-called ministry professionals to preach the gospel. Yes, God has gifted some in His church to be evangelists. But He has also called every one of us to evangelize regardless of whether we have that gift! Anyone can fill the role of a proclaimer. You don't need to be a full-time pastor, missionary, or evangelist. Being a truck driver, accountant, or secretary will do. You simply need to tell the people you meet about the good news of God's love for them.

It is a great mystery. For some reason God has chosen to make known His unsearchable riches in Christ through us. At some point, people must be confronted with the fact that they are sinners separated from a holy God. They must know that salvation is available in no other name than the name of Jesus Christ. They must know that by turning from their sins to Christ by faith they can have a personal relationship with God as well as the hope of eternal life.

You are the vehicle God has chosen to convey this great news to many of the unbelievers in your world. Don't question it. Accept it, and start sharing.

Jesus said, "The harvest truly is plentiful, but the laborers are few" (Matthew 9:37). He's looking for laborers. He wants you to be one. If you will say like the prophet Isaiah, "Lord, here I am; send me," just watch what He will do.

CHAPTER TEN

DISCIPLING
OTHERS

WE HAVE SEEN THAT HAVING a passion for Jesus sets others' hearts ablaze through the witness of the gospel. But like any fire, once started it must be maintained. It is not enough merely to lead a person into a relationship with Christ; it is also our duty to see that this relationship is strengthened. This is done through discipling.

Unfortunately, somewhere along the line we have separated evangelism from discipleship—even though there is no such distinction in Scripture. It is unbiblical simply to pray with someone to receive Christ, then say, "You're on your own. God bless you. See you around." We are to help new believers grow spiritually and become dedicated, committed, fruitful, and mature disciples of Jesus Christ. Only then will these new believers repeat the discipling process with others they lead to Christ. And so the discipleship cycle continues.

Saul's dramatic conversion on the Damascus Road (Acts 9:1-9) did not quell all doubt among other believers as to whether he had really become a Christian. Hadn't Saul been one of the prime persecutors of the early church?

Hadn't he presided over the execution of Stephen, the first Christian martyr in the New Testament? The disciples were afraid that Saul's "conversion" was just a ploy to find out where they met so he could turn them over to the authorities.

Saul's conversion was real, however, and God used a series of believers—including Barnabas and others—to prepare him for his work ahead. Acts 9:10-19 tells a very important part of Saul's story that is sometimes overlooked. In these verses we are introduced to a low-profile but very significant person in Saul's life:

> Now there was a certain disciple at Damascus named Ananias; and to him the Lord said in a vision, "Ananias."
> And he said, "Here I am, Lord."
> So the Lord said to him, "Arise and go to the street called Straight, and inquire at the house of Judas for one called Saul of Tarsus; for behold, he is praying. And in a vision he has seen a man named Ananias coming in and putting his hand on him, so that he might receive his sight."
> Then Ananias answered, "Lord, I have heard from many about this man, how much harm he has done to Your saints in Jerusalem. [Loose paraphrase: "Lord, are You sure You have the right guy here? This is *the* Saul of Tarsus?"] And here he has authority from the chief priests to bind all who call on Your name."
> But the Lord said to him, "Go, for he is a chosen vessel of Mine to bear My name before Gentiles, kings, and the children of Israel. For I will show him how many things he must suffer for My name's sake."
> And Ananias went his way, and entered the house; and laying his hands on him he said, "Brother Saul, the Lord Jesus, who appeared to you on the road as you came, has sent me that you may receive your sight and be filled with the Holy Spirit."

Immediately there fell from his eyes something like scales, and he received his sight at once; and he arose and was baptized. And when he had received food, he was strengthened. Then Saul spent some days with the disciples at Damascus.

Here we are introduced to a great hero of the church, a man named Ananias. "Ananias?" you say. "What great work did he do? Did he write any books in the New Testament? Did he perform any miracles? Can we read any of his sermons in the book of Acts?" No. But the man he discipled did all those things and far more. Little did Ananias know that the man he took under his wing would become the greatest preacher in the history of the Christian church.

The Ministry of Disciple-Making

What does it mean to disciple others? It's the process whereby you take a new believer under your care and influence to help him get on his feet spiritually. It doesn't mean teaching alone; it also means being an encouraging, supportive, prayerful friend. Tragically, I find that many people who receive Christ drift away from the church in the first few months because no one helps them to become established in the faith.

When I was a brand-new Christian, a young man came along and helped me get started in the faith. He had a dramatic effect on my life. I easily could have fallen through the cracks after I went forward to receive Jesus Christ as my Lord and Savior on my high school campus. I easily could have returned to my old lifestyle. But someone took the time to say to me, "Greg, I'm coming over to your house tonight to pick you up and take you to church with me." I doubt I ever would have gone on my own, but that person made sure I got to church and introduced me to other Christians.

After the services he would explain the meaning of some strange terms and answer my questions about the sermons. He discipled me the way Aquila and Priscilla discipled a new Christian named Apollos. Apollos was full of enthusiasm but lacking in instruction. So Aquila and Priscilla took him into their home and "explained to him the way of God more accurately" (Acts 18:26).

It's truly rewarding to take a new believer under your wing and watch him discover the truths of the Bible for the first time. I remember when the person who discipled me led me through a personal Bible study and I heard for the first time about Jesus' second coming. I couldn't believe it when he told me about the Rapture of the church. I thought, *You mean instead of going to heaven when I die, Jesus may come back for me in my lifetime?* My excitement fueled the same in my Christian friend.

New believers need to see how Christians live in the real world. They need someone to model the Christian life for them. It's great to sit with them in the pew and listen to the sermon together. But your example of Christian living outside the church building is just as important to their spiritual growth. New believers need to know how a Christian should treat his spouse and children. They need to see what Christians do for entertainment. What kind of movies do they attend? What do they watch on television? What kind of music do they listen to? What is their attitude toward life? New believers need someone to model the Christian life in daily living. That's what discipling is all about.

You might say, "That's precisely why I haven't taken a new Christian under my wing. I don't want them to see what my life is really like." If that's the case, maybe you need to make some changes in your activities, your conversation, or your thought life. Perhaps you are doing some things you shouldn't be doing. To be a discipler of others you need to be diligent about your own walk with the Lord.

Another roadblock that keeps Christians from actively discipling others is the fear that they don't know the Bible well enough. But it's not necessary that you be a Bible scholar to lead someone to Christ and disciple him or her. You may not be able to answer every question a new Christian poses, but you probably know a lot more about the Christian life than he does. You can begin by sharing the simple building blocks of the Christian life you already know: how to pray, how to read the Bible, how to get the most out of church, and how to live a godly life. Even as you are growing in Christ you can have a significant impact on the life of a new Christian.

Discipling Others Keeps You on Fire

Discipling benefits both the discipler and the disciple. Helping believers get grounded in the Word and involved in following Christ will encourage your own Christian life. As you add to the new believer's eagerness with your knowledge, wisdom, and experience, he will help keep your heart blazing with his passion and zeal.

That's why every church needs a constant flow of new believers. Without the refreshing zeal and excitement of new Christians, you have a dead or dying church. We stagnate spiritually when all we do is attend more Bible studies and prayer meetings, read more Christian books, and listen to more teaching tapes without an outlet for the truth we acquire. We need to take what God has given us and use it constructively in the lives of others. When new believers stream in, a church is energized, rejuvenating those of us who have been with the Lord for some time. And those of us who are more mature can help temper the new believer's zeal with the truth of the Scripture.

Children are a good illustration of this process. Being with children helps you see life through their eyes. As you help a child discover things for the first time, you rediscover the newness of those experiences. It's wonderful to watch a child discover the ocean—sifting the sand with his tiny fingers, listening to the roar of the waves, splashing in the water. It's exciting to see a child pick up snow or taste ice cream for the first time. We adults take these things for granted. But when we see a child discover them, we share in his excitement.

In the same way, we get excited when we see new believers discover truth and guidance while reading God's Word. We encourage each other when we uncover God's truth and put it into practice. Often new believers will ask us difficult questions that force us to search the Scriptures. These questions can help us rediscover (or discover for the first time) many important spiritual truths.

It's a scriptural principle that when we open ourselves to discipling others, we'll be encouraged and strengthened in return. Proverbs 11:25 says, "The generous soul will be made rich, and he who waters will also be watered himself." I have found that the more I give, the more God seems to give back to me.

At one point the children of Israel were facing the problem of spiritual stagnation. God told them through the prophet Isaiah to get their eyes off their own problems and start giving away what they had been given. Isaiah 58:6 says, "Is this not the fast that I have chosen: to loose the bonds of wickedness, to undo the heavy burdens, to let the oppressed go free, and that you break every yoke?" God's promise to them for being obedient is found in verse 8: "Then your light shall break forth like the morning, your healing shall spring forth speedily."

You can partake of this promise if you will open your life to disciple someone else. It can start today, right where you are and with the people God has brought into your life. For the sake of those who don't yet know Christ, don't forsake God's command to go and make disciples (Matthew 28:19). For the sake of the new believer, don't let apathy prevent you from blessing them through your loving care and guidance.

God's Divine Domino Effect

It's interesting that the Lord picked Ananias to disciple Saul. You have to understand that Saul was a "big catch" for such an ordinary believer. Notice that God did not choose Peter or one of the other apostles. The Lord bypassed people like James and John and used this little-known man named Ananias. Though Ananias is not usually remembered as a hero of the church, undoubtedly he made a difference at a crucial time in the discipling of Saul. Who knows if that person you are helping along, sharing with, or ministering to will not be the next apostle Paul?

Think of that great hero of the church, Edward Kimble. You've heard of him, haven't you? I doubt it. His name doesn't usually come to mind when we think of great luminaries of the church. Yet God used this ordinary man to touch off a string of events that would shake the world for Christ.

It all began when Edward Kimble felt the tugging of the Spirit to share his faith with a young shoe salesman he knew. At first Kimble vacillated, unsure if he should talk to the man. But he finally mustered his courage and went into the shoe store. There Kimble found the salesman in the back room stocking shoes, and he began to share his faith with him. As a result, the young shoe salesman prayed and received Jesus Christ that day. That shoe salesman's name was Dwight L. Moody, and he became the greatest evangelist of his generation.

But the story doesn't end there. Several years later a pastor and well-known author by the name of Frederick B. Meyer heard Moody preach. Meyer was so deeply stirred by Moody's preaching that he himself embarked on a far-reaching evangelistic ministry. Once when Meyer was preaching, a college student named Wilbur Chapman accepted Christ as a result of his presentation of the gospel. Chapman later employed a baseball player to help him prepare to conduct an evangelistic crusade. That ballplayer, who later became a powerful evangelist himself, was Billy Sunday.

Years later, a group of businessmen invited Billy Sunday to hold an evangelistic campaign in Charlotte, North Carolina, which resulted in many people coming to Christ. The businessmen were so touched by Sunday's preaching that they brought in another evangelist, Mordecai Ham, to hold another crusade. Ham's crusade went well, even though it did not have many converts. On one of the last nights of the meetings, however, one tall, lanky young man walked up the aisle to receive Christ. That man's name was Billy Graham.

Talk about a chain of events! And it all started with an ordinary Christian named Edward Kimble, who reached D.L. Moody, who reached Wilbur Chapman, who reached Billy Sunday, who reached Mordecai Ham, who reached Billy Graham. Look at what God has done over these many years because of the faithfulness of one person.

You just don't know if that person you're speaking to or discipling today might be the next D.L. Moody, Billy Graham, or apostle Paul. That's why you need to be faithful not only to lead others to Christ, but take them under your wing and disciple them to maturity. I often say about the process of discipling, it takes one to make one. Will you be one God can use to help new believers grow into mature disciples?

PART THREE

GUARDING
THE
PASSION

CHAPTER ELEVEN

WHEN OPPOSITION ROLLS IN

THE EARLY CHURCH HAD barely been set in motion before the devil launched his vicious campaign to try to bring its work to a halt. In Acts 3, perhaps only a few months after the Holy Spirit fell on the 120 in the upper room, Peter and John were used by God to heal the cripple at the temple gate. Though the masses were astounded by the miracle and 5000 people believed in Christ, the religious leaders of the day—the same people who were instrumental in Jesus' crucifixion—were upset by the apostles' teaching. They arrested Peter and John, interrogated them, threatened them, and then released them.

It was the first of many incidents of persecution to hit the church over the next decades. It marked the beginning of a period of great suffering for the church at the hands of the unbelieving Jewish religious leaders and Roman rulers. Some estimate that as many as six million Christians were put to death during this time of persecution.

Who was behind this persecution? Although Israel's religious leaders and Rome's emperors played key roles, clearly Satan masterminded the assault. Jesus described him as the thief in the sheepfold who only comes "to steal, and to kill, and to destroy" (John 10:10). Throughout the book of Acts we find that the devil used two primary methods of attack. He attacked the church outwardly through physical persecution, such as the arrest of the apostles in Acts 5, the beating of Paul and Silas in Acts 16, and the murder of Stephen in Acts 7 and James in Acts 12. And he attacked inwardly by infiltrating the church to cause dissension, as he did by convincing Ananias and Sapphira to lie to the Holy Spirit in Acts 5.

The enemy is still at it today. He continues to provoke the persecution of believers outwardly through people or circumstances. And he persecutes us inwardly by infiltrating our minds and tempting us to evil thoughts and deeds. His ultimate goal is to smother the passion that God has ignited within us and snuff out our effectiveness for Christ in this needy world.

For this reason we must keep up our guard and be aware of the methods and tactics he uses. As the apostle Paul said, "We are not ignorant of his devices" (2 Corinthians 2:11). Satan works in predictable patterns. He hasn't changed his tricks over the years, probably because they have worked so effectively. And if we are aware of his tactics, we can effectively ward off his attacks and guard the fire within us.

Persecution in the Life of the Believer

Every true follower of Jesus is going to be persecuted in some form. If you are really following Jesus Christ and living a godly life, the Bible promises that you will suffer some measure of persecution. Second Timothy 3:12 says, "All who desire to live godly in Christ Jesus will suffer persecution." If you've never been persecuted, maybe you're not living a godly life. The more you become like Him, the more others will lash out at you as a representative of God. Jesus Himself said, "'A servant is not greater than his master.' If they persecuted Me, they will also persecute you" (John 15:20).

Satan-inspired persecution can rear its ugly head in many ways. A family member may exclude you from gatherings because of your stand for Christ. A non-Christian neighbor or coworker may ignore you because of your beliefs. A boss may pass over you at promotion time because you will not compromise your integrity to win customers or increase profits through dishonest means. A teacher or administrator may ridicule you publicly for your stand against New Age curriculum or methods in your child's classroom. You may be made a laughingstock where you work or go to school because of your beliefs. It's even possible that your property may be vandalized and you may be physically assaulted because you stand up for Jesus Christ in your community. Whenever you are ignored, ridiculed, or attacked at any level for serving God and obeying His Word, you are the victim of persecution.

Fear of persecution causes some with a shallow commitment to abandon their faith. In the parable of the sower in Matthew 13, Jesus talked about the seed that fell on rocky ground and sprang up but soon withered and died since it had no root. Jesus then explained, "This is he who hears the word and immediately receives it with joy; yet he has no root in himself, but endures only for a while. For when tribulation or persecution arises because of the word, immediately he stumbles" (vv. 20,21).

When such a person reaches out to Jesus Christ, he is flooded with the emotion and excitement of the potential of a relationship with God. But when the Christian life demands any real commitment or Satan incites opposition, this excited but uncommitted person throws in the towel. Why? He doesn't like being persecuted. Such a person will never be a true follower of Jesus, because all who follow Him will be persecuted.

We need not fear the promised persecution. In fact, we can even be thankful for it. Yes, thankful! Let me give you at least three reasons for such a conviction.

First, *persecution is a blessing.* Jesus said, "Blessed are you when they revile and persecute you, and say all kinds of evil against you falsely for My sake. Rejoice and be exceedingly glad, for great is your reward in heaven, for so they persecuted the prophets who were before you" (Matthew 5:11,12). Jesus insists it's a privilege and a blessing to be persecuted and that a reward awaits us in heaven if we endure. So when you are being ridiculed for your faith, hang in there! To be identified with Jesus in any capacity is a great honor.

Second, *persecution is a purifier.* Persecution in the early church helped separate true believers from pretenders. Sincere followers of Jesus were strengthened as a result of persecution, while counterfeit or halfhearted members ran for the hills. The result? The entire church was purified. Likewise, if your commitment to Jesus Christ is genuine and sincere, persecution will not weaken you and your fellowship of believers; rather, it will strengthen you.

Third, *persecution reminds us of who we are and what the world is.* If you are being maligned or abused because of your faith in Christ and your stand for His Word, it should be a reminder to you that you are on the right course. Paul said all who live godly lives in Christ will be persecuted, so your pain should encourage you that your life is reflecting godliness. Furthermore, persecution shows us that the world under Satan's control is hostile to God and to us—and causes us to love the world less and love God more.

Persecution drives us into the open arms of Jesus, who welcomes us and comforts us.

Don't forget, either, that persecution will one day come to an end. Paul reminds us that "the sufferings of this present time are not worthy to be compared with the glory which shall be revealed in us" (Romans 8:18). The word he uses for "compare" is interesting because it was originally used in connection with weights. In this verse Paul suggests that when present suffering and persecution for the sake of our faith are put on the scales opposite future glory in Christ, there is no comparison. What awaits us in heaven far outweighs anything we suffer while serving Him here.

Paul uses the same analogy in 2 Corinthians 4:17: "For our light affliction, which is but for a moment, is working for us a far more exceeding and eternal weight of glory." Every pain of rejection and suffering should remind us of the great glory in Christ that lies ahead for us.

A Gain Worth the Pain

Perhaps the best-known case study of persecution in the early church is the experience of Stephen, whose faithfulness and fervor for Christ we've already noted. Though it's unlikely that any of us will suffer the ultimate in persecution—martyrdom—we can learn valuable lessons from this saint about being passionate for Christ no matter how we are opposed by those we seek to win. Let's examine the last day in the life of this man whom God so powerfully used.

In Acts 7 Stephen preached a powerful and convicting message to the religious leaders in Jerusalem. I don't know what kind of response Stephen expected from his audience, but he probably hoped it would be positive. I don't think he intentionally provoked the leaders of Israel to stone him. He desired to share the gospel with them. I'm sure he was deeply disappointed when they didn't respond favorably.

Stephen could tell his message wasn't going over well. He was reciting Israel's history and rebellion against God, and the ruling council resented it. No doubt their faces began to redden as Stephen gave them all a good history lesson. *How dare this young upstart tell us the meaning of Abraham, Moses, and the Law!* they probably thought. They missed the point of his message altogether. Stephen was speaking in the power of God's Spirit, but it just made them angry. Stephen could see the hostility rising.

Now, if Stephen had played his cards right, he could have gone home for dinner that night. He could have wrapped up his message by saying, "I can see you're not responsive to this message. It's obvious you are not interested in Jesus Christ as your Messiah. I don't want to say anything to offend you, so thank you very much for your kind attention. Now I really must be leaving."

Many of us would have taken such a tack, lovers of health and life that we are. But Stephen probably thought, *This is my one big shot with the Sanhedrin. This could be a hornet's nest, but if I could just reach one of them it will be worth it.* He might have even looked at Saul of Tarsus and thought, *God could even reach him through what I say.* So Stephen went for the jugular. He pulled out the stops and gave it his all.

Let me forewarn you: If you are looking to make friends when you share the gospel, you may want to avoid concluding the way Stephen did: "You stiff-necked and uncircumcised in heart and ears! You always resist the Holy Spirit; as your fathers did, so do you. Which of the prophets did your fathers not persecute? And they killed those who foretold the coming of the Just One, of whom you now have become the betrayers and murderers, who have received the law by the direction of angels and have not kept it" (vv. 51-53).

The Holy Spirit had these religious leaders under heavy conviction, but instead of yielding they became so angry they could hardly speak. They were livid. Then Stephen stoked their wrath even hotter. Being full of the Holy Spirit, he gazed into heaven and saw the glory of God with Jesus standing at the right hand of God. Instead of keeping it to himself, he exclaimed, "Look! I see the heavens opened and the Son of Man standing at the right hand of God!" (v. 56). The leaders shrieked with anger, bolted out of their seats, seized Stephen, dragged him outside the city, and stoned him to death for telling them the truth.

Notice that Stephen didn't intentionally goad the members of the Sanhedrin to anger and murder. He was simply proclaiming the truth in the power of the Holy Spirit as God directed him—and on this occasion it resulted in martyrdom.

Some folks don't feel they have adequately presented or defended the gospel unless they provoke someone to an angry response. But we're not told to speak the truth until it angers people; we're to speak the truth in love (Ephesians 4:15). Badgering people with the gospel until they cuss you out or take a swing at you is wrong—*unless*, as in Stephen's case, God's Spirit directs you to make such a pointed confrontation.

On the other hand, some Christians are so paranoid about offending unbelievers with the gospel that they water down their witness until it hardly makes an impact. Our call is not to preach the gospel to every creature until it upsets them, then back off or change the subject. Our call is to preach the gospel in the power of the Holy Spirit and under His direction. If your presentation happens to make somebody mad, it's okay. You certainly want to be as pleasing and winsome as possible to everyone you speak to about Christ. But when your faith is under fire, don't back down or soft-peddle your message to please your hearers. You are responsible to please God alone.

When someone rejects you and your message, you may be tempted to a defensive, sour-grapes attitude that says, "Too bad for you. God is going to get you for treating me that way." But Stephen's example in the last moments of his life shows that we must have a much different attitude toward those who reject us and persecute us. He knelt down and cried with a loud voice, "Lord, do not charge them with this sin" (v. 60). His words are similar to those of Jesus on the cross: "Father, forgive them, for they do not know what they do" (Luke 23:34). We are to forgive the unbelievers who reject us and regard them with love.

One Life to Live

Does the story of Stephen seem to be a real tragedy? After all, he lived so few years. But look at what was accomplished in the life of a young man named Saul who guarded the coats of those who stoned Stephen! In God's economy, the quality of a life outweighs the number of years. We must be ready to live for Him and proclaim Him even if it costs us our life.

In 1948 another young man named Jim Elliot wrote these words in his journal: "I seek not a long life, but a full one like You, Lord Jesus." Jim Elliot was in many ways a modern-day Stephen. Fresh out of college, he felt called by God to South America where he aimed to preach the gospel to a group of Indians known as the Aucas. He and his friends flew down and made contact with these spiritually needy people, dropping little presents from the plane in hopes of building rapport until they could share more about Jesus Christ.

Finally they felt the time had come to make contact. Their wives anxiously waited nearby, listening by radio to

hear what happened. Jim and the others set a time to contact them. But when that time came and went, the women
grew worried and sent help into the jungle to see what had
happened.

When the search party found the plane with the skin
torn off its wings, they realized something awful had happened. Then they discovered the bodies of the five missionaries who had been brutally killed by the Aucas. They
found the body of Jim Elliot thrust through with a spear, a
gospel tract wrapped around the shaft. Jim laid down his
life for the sake of the gospel. Just as he wrote in his journal, Jim indeed lived a short life, but a full one.

The story doesn't end there, however. Jim's wife
Elisabeth had the courage to go back to this tribe with the
same message her husband preached. Amazingly, she had
the privilege of personally leading to faith in Christ the
very man who threw the spear that killed her husband.
This inspiring story is contained in Elisabeth Elliot's book,
Through Gates of Splendor.

Many Christians today seem to care more about a long
life than the full life Jim Elliot so desired. A long life *can* be
a full life, but as Stephen and Jim Elliot illustrate, life doesn't
need to be long to be full. You weren't born with a written
guarantee attached to your toe promising 90 years of life. But
God did promise you abundant life (John 10:10). That's what
I want: a full life that honors God no matter how many—or
few—years I may have. I trust you want the same, regardless
of any persecution you may suffer as a result of serving Christ.

The Persecution that Backfired

Some remarkable things happened to the church in
Jerusalem after Stephen's death. Acts 8:1 says, "At that
time a great persecution arose against the church which

was at Jerusalem; and they were all scattered throughout the regions of Judea and Samaria, except the apostles."

Up to this point the church had been bogged down in Jerusalem. Jesus had told the disciples in Acts 1:8 that they would be His witnesses in Jerusalem, and in all Judea and Samaria, and to the end of the earth. But they were still nestled comfortably in Jerusalem.

This "holy huddle" didn't last long after Stephen's death. God allowed persecution from the hand of Saul in order to fan out the church and take the gospel to more regions than before. Like seeds cast to the wind, thousands of believers fled Jerusalem for their lives, taking the good news to Judea and Samaria where it took root and grew in the lives of others.

We never know what God has in mind when He allows us to be persecuted for the sake of our faith. Stephen's life was snuffed out—but his life had a profound impact on at least one person who in turn reached countless thousands: Saul of Tarsus. Jim Elliot's life was brief—but who knows if the Aucas would have been reached any other way? And how many other young men and women have committed their lives to the ministry of evangelism in response to Jim Elliot's life and death?

Perhaps your boss has demoted you or transferred you out of his department because of your stand for Christ. On the surface it may seem a tragedy. But think about the opportunities to share your faith when fellow workers in your new department ask, "Why were you transferred here?" Or suppose you have been given the cold shoulder by the neighborhood coffee klatch because they don't want a Christian around while they dish their dirt. Maybe this is your chance to get some other neighborhood women together for coffee and an evangelistic Bible study.

Persecution doesn't thwart God's plans for you in the least. In fact, sometimes persecution opens doors that could be opened in no other way. Instead of feeling defeated when you are verbally or physically abused for your faith, thank God for the new avenues of service He is about to open as a result of this difficulty.

Time for a Refilling

May I point out one more unique quality in the persecuted early believers? In Acts 4 Peter and John were arrested and told not to preach anymore. After their release they returned to the other believers and had a prayer meeting. What did they pray for? Protection? No. Judgment upon those who had threatened them? No. They prayed, "Lord, we need more boldness." More boldness? Isn't that what got Peter and John into trouble in the first place? Yet they wanted more boldness because preaching Christ was more important to them than any trouble it might cause for them. That should be our response to persecution no matter how slight or how painful it may be.

After the disciples prayed for greater boldness, God refilled them with His Spirit. In the same way, God wants to refill us with the power of His Spirit that we may share Christ boldly. We constantly need to be refilled, but we sometimes forget; persecution reminds us of the necessity! Ephesians 5:18 exhorts, "Be filled with the Spirit," which literally means "be *constantly* filled with the Spirit." Being filled with the Holy Spirit is not a one-time event. It's an ongoing process.

Moreover, the original Greek in this verse is in the imperative. God does not *suggest* that you be filled with the Spirit; He *commands* it. He wants you to take hold of all the resources He has made available to you. And as you open yourself to His Spirit daily, He will fill you and give you boldness to serve Him in the face of any persecution that may come your way. He will keep your passion burning brightly.

CHAPTER TWELVE

RISING ABOVE TRYING CIRCUMSTANCES

SO YOU THINK YOU'VE GOT problems? Imagine yourself with your back bloodied and stinging with pain after having been whipped. Your legs are tightly shackled and spread as far apart as possible, causing excruciating pain. And you're locked in a musty, cold, dark cave. What would you do in such a dilemma? Scream? Cry? Get angry at God?

The book of Acts tells us Paul and Silas found themselves in precisely those circumstances, yet they were able to rise above their problems and even witness to those around them. Their example will help us see how God can use difficult situations to make us stronger and more like Him. Instead of being turned upside down by our trials, we can learn to respond positively to them and become men and women who turn our world rightside up for Jesus Christ.

During a missionary tour through Asia, Paul and Silas came into Philippi to share the life-changing message about Jesus Christ. The story is told in Acts 16. They went to a river and began to share the gospel, first with an affluent woman named Lydia. Despite her financial position and influence, her life was empty. As Paul shared the gospel, Lydia discovered the answer she had been searching for. She and her family made a public commitment to Jesus Christ and were baptized.

Whenever God works, Satan tries to strike back and uproot what the Spirit is doing. With the ministry in Philippi off to such a promising start, Satan began his counterattack. A demon-possessed girl who told fortunes began to follow Paul and Silas around the city saying, "These men are the servants of the Most High God" (Acts 16:17). This was a strange tactic indeed! Perhaps it would have made more sense if the girl had opposed their message. But by affirming it she probably caused some people to think she was one of them, thus confusing those who knew that the girl was involved in the occult.

Flooding the world with cheap imitations of Christianity is one of the devil's favorite tactics. Unquestionably, it works. So many bizarre cults and religious groups throughout the world today mention just enough of Jesus Christ to cause many unbelievers to recoil when the real gospel is presented.

After awhile, Paul became annoyed with the girl's interruptions. He spun around, rebuked the demon in her, and cast it out.

The Hardship That Comes with Obedience

Paul's ministry to the girl created a major problem for her masters, however, for she had brought in large amounts of money through her demonic fortune-telling. Because of Paul, these men were now out of business—and they wanted him punished. They brought Paul and Silas before the crowd and accused them of bringing a false religion to their city. The angry crowd accosted Paul and Silas, beat them with rods, and cast them into a dungeon.

Christianity is often bad for some kinds of businesses, especially those that trade in human weakness. Wherever God's servants live the genuine Christian life, they create a disturbance.

So many people came to faith in Jesus Christ during some of the great American revivals that bars were shut down due to lack of business. Police officers were laid off because there wasn't enough crime to keep them busy. Incredible, isn't it? Can you imagine something like that happening today? Crime and immorality greatly reduced because of obedience to the gospel? That's what I mean by seeing the world turned rightside up. God can do it again as we allow ourselves to be lit on fire for Him.

Once I was in Sacramento, California, for an evangelistic crusade and a newspaper reporter asked me, "I've been reading research that says young people are turning away from organized religion in droves. Have you found that fewer young people are attending your crusades?"

I said, "No, I've found the opposite to be true. We're seeing more young people than ever before."

"Why do your crusades attract so many young people while other churches are seeing such a decline?" he asked.

"I think the answer is in the phrase you used: organized religion. Organized religion isn't reaching the young people attending our crusades, because they aren't looking for religion. They're looking for a relationship with Jesus Christ, and that's what we are offering."

Had Paul and Silas conformed to organized religion in Philippi they probably would not have found themselves in a Philippian jail. But they did not go on this journey to make friends; they went to make disciples of Christ. And now, like their Savior, they were suffering for their message.

Though few of us may be called upon to suffer so severely, we all suffer difficulties and trials as a result of taking a stand for Christ. If we allow negative circumstances to get us down, Satan's strategy has worked. We need to know how to rise above these trying times and burn even brighter for Christ as a result. Paul and Silas knew just how to do it.

Songs in the Night

Here were Paul and Silas, stuffed into a dark, smelly cave, legs racked with pain, backs ripped open by Roman whips. What did they do? What would *you* do? It would be easy to question God in such circumstances. "Excuse me, Lord, but are you paying attention up there? How could you let this happen to me? Somehow this just doesn't go along with what I pictured the Christian life to be. What's wrong here?"

They could have become angry at God—but instead we read that they sang and rejoiced: "At midnight Paul and Silas were praying and singing hymns to God, and the prisoners were listening to them" (Acts 16:25). Instead of groans, songs issued from their mouths. Instead of cursing the men who had them arrested, they blessed God. Instead of complaining or calling on God to judge those who had inflicted their pain, Paul and Silas prayed. No wonder the other prisoners were listening to them. Never before had they heard such sounds ringing through the prison.

When you are in pain, the midnight hour may not feel like the best time for a worship service. Nevertheless, as it says in the book of Job, "God my Maker . . . gives songs in the night" (35:10). Psalm 42:8 says, "The Lord will command His lovingkindness in the daytime, and in the night His song shall be with me—a prayer to the God of my life."

That's why in the midst of a bleak, difficult set of circumstances, Paul and Silas could rejoice.

C.H. Spurgeon said, "Any fool can sing in the day. It's
easier to sing when we read the notes by daylight. But the
skillful singer is he who can sing when there is not a ray of
light to read by. Songs in the night come only from God.
They are not in the power of men."

Paul and Silas' midnight song brings to mind the fasci-
nating story in 2 Chronicles 20 in which God gave King
Jehoshaphat one of the strangest battle plans of all time.
Knowing that the enemy army was moving in on his
nation, Jehoshaphat, in obedience to the Lord, sent singers
ahead of his army to "sing to the Lord, and . . . praise the
beauty of holiness" (v. 21).

If you had been a musician in Judah, you might not
have been real excited about performing that day. A harp
and a flute aren't the most potent weapons to take into the
heat of battle! On the other hand, it might have been a
good opportunity to get rid of all the people who sang too
loudly or played off-key! God's strange instructions were
intended to show Jehoshaphat that victory only comes by
His Spirit, not by weapons and armies.

As the singers began to sing, 2 Chronicles 20:22
records, "The Lord sent ambushes against the [enemy]."
Caught by surprise and utterly confused, the invading soldiers began to attack and kill each other. Through this
remarkable victory the people not only learned the
dynamic of rising above their circumstances, but recognized that praise and worship are vital elements in spiritual
warfare.

Our evangelistic crusades utilize contemporary praise
and worship music to prepare the hearts of the people for
the message of the gospel. God can powerfully use wor-
shipful, Christ-honoring music in evangelism. This world
has nothing like the praise and worship music we sing. In

fact, outside the church there are very few times people sing together. At a ball game the crowd may sing the national anthem, or at a concert they may join in on an old, familiar song. Yet the music of worship and praise is unique to the church alone.

Psalm 22:3 reminds us that God inhabits the praises of His people. Jesus told us, "Where two or three are gathered together in My name, I am there in the midst of them" (Matthew 18:20). When an unbeliever comes into a Spirit-empowered, biblically grounded worship service, the music can dramatically impact his life. He may be touched spiritually by seeing and hearing God's people in loving communion with their Lord.

I distinctly remember the first time I saw Christians worshiping the Lord together. I sensed the presence of God in that meeting and I could see that the relationship these people had with Jesus Christ was real and genuine. It touched me deeply, thus preparing my heart for the message to follow from the Word of God. I discovered through the worship that God was real and could be approached and known. I was then vitally interested in approaching Him and knowing Him for myself.

We see the same dynamic of worship in spiritual battle when David sang for King Saul. Whenever an evil spirit tormented King Saul, he called for David, who played his harp and worshiped the Lord. David's music caused the spirit to leave Saul for a time. Playing for Saul was risky business, however. On one occasion Saul picked up his spear and threw it at David. But as David worshiped God, his songs of praise and adoration had an impact on the forces of darkness.

Rejoicing Lifts You Above Your Circumstances

When I say "rising above our circumstances," I'm not talking about mind over matter. I'm talking about faith over circumstances. I'm saying that no matter what the circumstances are, God is in control of every detail of your life as a Christian. The word "oops" is not in His vocabulary. Aren't you glad of that? He knows what He's doing. He promises, "All things work together for good to those who love God, to those who are the called according to His purpose" (Romans 8:28).

About this wonderful and oft-quoted verse, Roy Laurin wrote in his commentary on Romans:

> Here is a place where all life's events pass a point of providence. Here they are resolved to fit a pre-arranged and predetermined goal. That goal is "for good." Here is a conviction which will give a new complexion to life. It will give equilibrium in the midst of storm; poise in the midst of distress; faith in the midst of doubt; courage in the midst of danger; and hope in the midst of despair. Here life is removed from the fateful fruits of accidents and has a fixed purpose. The ultimate end of that purpose is good, although its immediate means may appear calamitous.

This promise states that *all* things, whatever their color or character, work together for good. David, recognizing this principle, wrote, "All [things] are Your servants" (Psalm 119:91). All the seasons—cold and heat, snow and rain, frost and sunshine—work together from seemingly opposite directions to produce a good crop. God does the same with all things in the life of His children.

Does this mean that everything that happens to us is good in and of itself? Hardly. Many things are not good. They may even be painful and bitter. Ultimately, however, God's divine purpose causes everything to resolve into good. I've seen the death of a loved one bring many to Christ who previously had no interest in the gospel. I've seen suffering and sickness bring unbelievers and prodigals to their spiritual senses.

The writer of Psalm 119 acknowledges that the Lord used suffering to strengthen him spiritually: "Before I was afflicted I went astray, but now I keep Your word" (v. 67); "It is good for me that I have been afflicted, that I may learn Your statutes" (v. 71); "I know, O Lord, that Your judgments are right, and that in faithfulness You have afflicted me" (v. 75). The old Puritan Thomas Watson observed, "A sick-bed often teaches more than a sermon."

The phrase "work together" in Romans 8:28 equates to the English word "synergism," which means the working together of various elements to produce an effect greater than, and often completely different than, the sum of each element acting separately. In the physical world, the right combination of otherwise harmful chemicals can produce beneficial substances. If you combine the two poisons sodium and chlorine, for example, you get ordinary table salt. In the same way, some unfortunate elements of life can be combined to produce something valuable. David reflects this truth when he writes, "All the paths of the Lord are mercy and truth, to such as keep His covenant and His testimonies" (Psalm 25:10).

Moreover, the phrase "all things work together" is better translated "all things *are working* together." There are no breaks or lapses in God's plan for things working together for good. He doesn't work for good in some things but not in others. He doesn't work today, then take tomorrow off.

Sometimes when the bottom drops out, we wonder if the Lord is asleep on the watch. But the Scriptures remind us, "He who keeps Israel shall neither slumber nor sleep" (Psalm 121:4). He is available to you 24 hours a day! He will take care of you. He will either deliver you from the situation or see you through it. If He allows you to go through it, be assured He has a plan. Realizing this truth, Paul and Silas called on the Lord and worshiped Him, rising above their miserable circumstances.

It's amazing that when you begin to worship the Lord in tough circumstances, your problems are a little easier to handle. Why? Because when you worship, you are acknowledging the greatness of God. When you recognize how big God is, your problems come back into perspective. When we take our eyes off the Lord and fix them on our problems, we feel overwhelmed and worry up a storm. When you realize God is in control and begin to worship Him, you will soar above your circumstances, just as Paul and Silas did.

The Concert That Brought the House Down

As Paul and Silas sang into the night, a great earthquake shook the foundations of the prison. This was no ordinary earthquake, because chains fell off the prisoners and the doors were opened, yet no one was harmed. We don't read that Paul and Silas prayed for an earthquake or even for deliverance. They just prayed and sang hymns to God. God sent a supernatural earthquake custom-designed for them.

We can say this is a great story of God's deliverance, but I don't think deliverance is the primary focus of the story. As far as I can see, the focus of the story is rejoicing in trying circumstances. You see, the earthquake doesn't always come. Sometimes God takes us *out of* our problems, but many times He simply takes us *through* them. We need to rejoice and praise God not so He will take away the pain, but because He is in control whether He delivers us or not.

Three or four years after the earthshaking incident in Philippi, Paul was imprisoned again for preaching the gospel.

But this time there was no earthquake. Instead he spent his time writing to the jailer and to all the other believers in the church in Philippi. It was a letter of joy and rejoicing from beginning to end: "Rejoice in the Lord always. Again I will say, rejoice! Let your gentleness be known to all men. The Lord is at hand. Be anxious for nothing, but in everything by prayer and supplication, with thanksgiving, let your requests be made known to God; and the peace of God, which passes all understanding, will guard your hearts and minds through Christ Jesus" (Philippians 4:4-7).

I appreciate knowing that Paul wrote those words in prison. Had he written them in a palace, they wouldn't have as great an impact upon me. But he wrote them in dire straits.

Paul's final letter, 2 Timothy, also was written from prison. Again, no angel delivered him as Peter had been delivered. No earthquake came this time as in Philippi. In fact, he was awaiting execution by beheading. But he was still singing songs in the night: "For I am already being poured out as a drink offering, and the time of my departure is at hand. I have fought the good fight, I have finished the race, I have kept the faith. Finally, there is laid up for me the crown of righteousness, which the Lord, the righteous Judge, will give to me on that Day, and not to me only but also to all who have loved His appearing" (2 Timothy 4:6-8).

As you trust God and worship Him in the midst of your trials, the earthquake of deliverance may or may not come. God may airlift you out of the problem you're in, or He may just leave you in it and send you the strength you need to endure. Either way, God is with you. He will deliver you out of it or sustain you through it. And for that He's worthy of our songs of praise.

A child of God who rejoices in difficult circumstances serves as a mighty witness to unbelievers. The other prisoners were listening to Paul and Silas singing. In the

Greek, the word "listening" used in Acts 16 actually means listening with great attention and pleasure. Have you ever listened to a piece of music that seemed flawless and you enjoyed every moment of it? That's the kind of listening described in this passage. Every prisoner was listening, taking in every word.

When the earthquake came, the jailer was ready to kill himself because Roman law mandated that he receive the same punishment as his prisoners if he allowed them to escape. So he pulled out his sword and was ready to thrust it into himself when Paul cried out, "Do yourself no harm." Now, if Paul had wanted to get back at the jailer for mistreating him, this would have been the perfect opportunity. "Go for it," he could have said. "You deserve it after what you did to Silas and me. Take your own life."

But Paul and Silas had compassion for the jailer. It's possible their earlier prayers may have been for him. Perhaps Paul related to the jailer, knowing what it's like to be governed by hate. Don't forget, before his conversion Paul used to be the dreaded Saul of Tarsus who tortured and imprisoned believers.

The jailer was so touched by Paul's actions that he said, "What must I do to be saved?" Thank God when an unbeliever comes up to you and says, "What makes you so different? What makes you tick? I want to know more about it. I've seen you read your Bible. I've seen you pray. But more importantly, I've seen your attitude and your actions at work. I've seen the way you treat your family. I've seen your peace and joy. I want what you've got. What do I have to do to be like you?" That's the greatest of all compliments.

Paul and Silas were able to minister the truth to the jailer and he was converted. Then the jailer, having been washed clean by Jesus Christ, washed the wounds of Paul and Silas to show his thankfulness for what God had done for him. But it all began when two servants of God in a tough spot decided to praise God and trust Him to work out His plan in their situation. Think of what God can do in and through you as you learn to respond to your difficulties this way!

There is a story about an elderly pastor who spent a great deal of time ministering to the sick and distressed people in his congregation. He always carried in his Bible an old bookmark made of silk threads. On one side of the bookmark the threads were woven into a beautiful motto. But on the back the threads looked like a tangled mess.

Whenever the old preacher called on someone who was distressed by a nasty turn of events, he placed the bookmark in the person's hand with the tangled side up. "What do you think of this?" he would ask.

The person often responded, "This is nothing more than a jumble of threads."

Then the pastor turned the bookmark over so the anguished individual could read the message the threads produced: *God is love.* "Right now your life looks like the back of the bookmark," he would say. "But be assured that God has a beautiful message of His love in your circumstances for you and for others."

It may be that right now you see only the back of the bookmark. But your heavenly Father is working all things together for good in your life. Like Paul and Silas, sing songs of praise in the night, and you will eventually see God's goodness in your circumstance.

CHAPTER THIRTEEN

CHRIST'S CALL
TO COURAGE

HAVE YOU EVER BEEN discouraged as a Christian or felt like a failure? Are you frightened about the future? Take heart! You are not the first child of God to feel this way and I'm sure you won't be the last. In fact, even members of that dynamic early church—including none other than the great apostle Paul— struggled with discouragement and fear. Yet Jesus revived Paul when he was down and called him to courage. I believe what Jesus did for Paul will bring courage to you as well in moments of discouragement and fear that threaten to smother your passion for God.

Toward the end of his ministry, Paul started out on what would be his final trip to Jerusalem. He believed it was the Lord's will for him to go there. He boarded a ship in Ephesus and stopped for a time in Caesarea to visit Philip the evangelist, his friend and fellow believer.

During his stay Paul met a colorful prophet named Agabus. In dramatic fashion, Agabus bound his own hands and feet with Paul's belt and prophesied, "So shall the Jews at Jerusalem bind the man who owns this belt, and deliver him into the hands of the Gentiles" (Acts 21:11). The other believers, realizing what awaited their beloved Paul, pleaded tearfully with him not to go. Paul responded, "What do you mean by weeping and breaking my heart? For I am ready not only to be bound, but also to die at Jerusalem for the name of the Lord Jesus" (v. 13). Determined to go to Jerusalem and proclaim the gospel, Paul ignored the warning of Agabus and the emotional pleas of the other disciples.

This incident has led many to wonder if Paul was really led by the Lord to go to Jerusalem. What if the warning from Agabus and the opposition from Paul's friends was God's way of saying, "Paul, you're on the wrong track. Don't go to Jerusalem"? Was Paul obeying the inner direction of the Holy Spirit to go to Jerusalem or unwittingly rejecting God's primary plan for him in his enthusiasm to preach the gospel?

Personally, I think Paul was in God's will. The Lord was simply preparing him for what awaited him. Whether he was in the center of God's will or not, you have to give him credit for his determination to preach the gospel. You have to admire the resolve of a man who knows that imprisonment is awaiting him, yet continues to hold his course.

Let's say that you felt called by the Lord to visit a certain city to proclaim the gospel, but a respected Christian friend told you that if you went, you would be arrested and jailed. Would you still go? Or would you begin to doubt God's will about going? Paul was determined to go ahead despite the threat of opposition because he believed God wanted him to bear witness of the gospel in Jerusalem. And so he went.

Sure enough, soon after he arrived and began preaching, the Jews became angry. Just as Agabus prophesied, Paul was delivered "into the hands of the Gentiles," the Roman authorities: "And when there arose a great dissension, the [Roman] commander, fearing lest Paul might be pulled to pieces by them, commanded the soldiers to go down and take him by force from among them, and bring him into the barracks" (Acts 23:10).

Roman soldiers took Paul to Antonio's Fortress, a fortified prison originally built by Mark Anthony that still exists today.

Be Encouraged!

It was in these bleak surroundings that the discouraged Paul was visited by his Lord: "But the following night the Lord stood by him and said, 'Be of good cheer, Paul; for as you have testified for Me in Jerusalem, so you must also bear witness at Rome'" (v. 11).

Why am I so sure that Paul was discouraged and probably frightened? Because the first words of Jesus were, "Be of good cheer." Whenever an angel or the Lord Himself appeared to someone and said, "Don't be afraid" or "Be of good cheer," it most likely meant that person was afraid or discouraged. The Lord's initial greeting always corresponded to the person's condition at that moment. And in this case, He wanted to bring courage to Paul's discouraged heart.

From a human standpoint, how *could* Paul "be of good cheer" in a dark, damp Roman dungeon with a band of angry Jews outside just waiting to kill him? A careful examination of the Lord's words gives us the answer. God did not bring Paul a shallow greeting like "Laugh and be happy, Paul" or "Have a nice day!" A more literal translation of "Be of good cheer" is "Be encouraged." The Lord didn't appear to Paul merely to bring him a smile, but to bring him courage for his circumstances and uncertain future.

Maybe you are discouraged right now or even frightened about your future. Perhaps your commitment to share the gospel in your neighborhood or workplace is meeting stiff resistance. I believe Jesus' encouraging words to Paul will bring comfort to you as well. How does Jesus bring courage to our hearts? We find the answer in Acts 23:11: "The Lord stood by [Paul] and said, 'Be of good cheer [or courage], Paul; for as you have testified for Me in Jerusalem, so you must also bear witness at Rome.'"

1. The Lord stands by us. First, note that the Lord stood by Paul. Yes, the Lord was there with Paul in that prison cell. Sadly, the local believers were not present to comfort Paul—at least we don't read of their presence. But the Lord came to visit him in that dark dungeon.

C.H. Spurgeon, speaking of this verse, said, "If all else forsook [Paul] Jesus was company enough. If all others despised him, the smile of Jesus was approval enough. If the good cause seemed to be in danger, in the presence of the Master, victory was sure. The Lord who had stood for him at the cross now stood for him in the prison. It was a dungeon, but the Lord was there. It was dark, but the glory of the Lord lit it up with heaven's own splendor. Better to be in a jail with the Lord than to be anywhere else without Him."

What more could Paul ask for! And what a comfort it is to know that, just as Jesus stood by Paul in his time of need, He will stand by each of us in ours.

Some years ago I was asked to speak to a group of Christians in the Philippines. Upon arriving in Manila, I was told that the meeting was to be held on the island of Mindanao. The day before I left I attended a prayer break-fast with some Filipino pastors. A couple of them heard of my plans to go to Mindanao and commended me for my bravery. When I asked why, they told me that ten pastors had recently been shot down in cold blood while preaching there. Suddenly, my trip didn't seem like such a good idea!

To make matters worse, the person who zealously arranged the meeting on this embattled island had a "last-minute change in plans" and was unable to accompany me. Furthermore, he arranged for me to fly there on a military transport. This was another problem, because an uprising among the rebels on the island resulted in great hostility toward the government. As the plane took off, I was suddenly gripped by fear as I anticipated being blown out of the sky or shot while preaching. I thought, *This could easily be the end for me.*

I turned to Scripture for consolation and happened upon Psalm 139. These words leaped out at me: "If I take the wings of the morning, and dwell in the uttermost parts of the sea, even there Your hand shall lead me, and Your right hand shall hold me" (vv. 9,10). As I looked out the plane's window, listening to the drone of the engines, I could see the morning sun beginning to rise. I was reassured that God was with me as I took "the wings of the morning" to a pretty undesirable speaking engagement, and He would see me through, which He did.

No matter where we are or what we are facing, God's Word promises that He is right there with us.

2. The Lord understands our situation. Jesus not only brought courage to Paul with His presence, but also with the assurance that He knew exactly where Paul was and what he was going through. Paul may have been shut up in Antonio's Fortress out of public view, but Jesus was fully aware of where he was and visited him there.

In the same way, God knows everything about us and where we are at all times. God is with us in the prisons of our lives. For some, it may be a literal prison. I often get letters from prisoners who write to tell me what God is doing in them and through them there in their prison cells.

Others find themselves in the "prison" of a hospital room or convalescent home. They would love to get out of their sick beds or wheelchairs and do what they want to do, but they are confined for a time. It's like a prison, but God is right there with them and understands their situation.

The Lord is with you no matter what you are going through. He understands what you are experiencing. Hebrews 4:15,16 says, "For we do not have a High Priest who cannot sympathize with our weaknesses, but was in all points tempted as we are, yet without sin. Let us therefore come boldly to the throne of grace, that we may obtain mercy and find grace to help in time of need." You have a God who knows what it's like to walk in a human body. He knows what it's like to face the pressures you face, and He is understanding and compassionate.

Moreover, He knows what you will face in the future. Jesus knew exactly what awaited Paul and He was there to brace him for the future by giving him a special touch. Paul didn't know that 40 men had taken a vow not to eat or drink until he was dead (Acts 23:12,13). Knowing about 40 would-be assassins would no doubt have made Paul's life more miserable than it already was, so God just lovingly kept that information from him. Paul didn't need to know it. All he needed to know was that Jesus was with him and understood his situation.

Sometimes we wish God would reveal the future to us and we wonder why He doesn't. But many times it's best that we don't know what's ahead. It could be frightening. God reveals to us as much as we need to know at any given moment. He knew what Paul was going to face and He prepared him for it. Likewise, He is preparing you and equipping you for what lies ahead. As Spurgeon said, "The Lord knows all about your troubles before they come to you. He anticipates them by His tender foresight. Before Satan can draw the bow, the Preserver of men will put His beloved beyond the reach of the arrow. Before the weapon is forged in the furnace and prepared on the anvil, He knows how to provide us with armor of proof which shall blunt the edge of the sword and break the point of the spear."

God knows exactly what's coming in your life. He sees what is happening in the enemy's camp. He sees the weapons that are being formed against you and He is already preparing His defense for you. Isaiah 54:17 assures us, "'No weapon formed against you shall prosper, and every tongue which rises against you in judgment you shall condemn. This is the heritage of the servants of the Lord, and their righteousness is from Me,' says the Lord."

3. The Lord affirms our work. Jesus did something else to bring courage to Paul's frightened heart. He said, "You testified of Me in Jerusalem." Jesus reminded Paul that He knew of his labor for Him in Jerusalem and approved of it.

As I said, I don't know if Paul was in God's will by going to Jerusalem. As Paul sat in his dark prison cell, he may have second-guessed his decision. He may have thought, *Agabus was right. His warning must have been from the Lord. I should have listened to him. My friends were right, too. They wept and asked me not to go to Jerusalem. I ignored them, and here I am in this stinking prison when I could be out preaching the gospel. I must have missed God's will.* No doubt the devil was right there, just pounding into him, "You've failed and let God down. God will never use you again. Just give up. You're going to die tomorrow."

But Jesus appeared to Paul and said, "Be encouraged, Paul. I'm here with you, and I know you came to Jerusalem to testify of Me." Jesus recognized Paul's faithfulness and his desire to please Him and commended him for it.

Similarly, even when we are unsure of the will of God, the Lord still looks at our hearts and our faithfulness to Him. This is confirmed in Jesus' words to the sick and recovering church at Philadelphia in the book of Revelation: "I know your works. . . . You have a little strength, have kept My word, and have not denied My name" (3:8). There were many reasons He could have criticized the church at Philadelphia.

But He said, "At least you have kept My Word and haven't denied My name. You're not completely mature and obedient, but you're making an effort."

Jesus knows when we need correction and He also knows when we need encouragement. When we cross the line, God corrects us; but He also approves us for what we have done right. When God acknowledged Paul's work in Jerusalem, He seemed to be saying, "Paul, your ministry is not judged as much by your success as by your faithfulness." In the same way, God looks at the motive behind our work even if it appears to be a failure to us or those around us.

4. God promises us further ministry. After assuring Paul of His presence and understanding and affirming his ministry in Jerusalem, the Lord further encouraged the apostle by saying, "You must also bear witness at Rome." Hearing this, Paul must have deduced, "If I'm going to bear witness in Rome, that means I'm getting out of this prison, and that's good news." More importantly, it meant that God had more work for Paul to do.

Perhaps you have looked at your past with regret, wondering if you've missed God's will for your life. I have good news for you. You have another chance. Just as God had additional ministry and opportunities for Paul in Rome, so He has the same for you. No, you can't change the past any more than you can unscramble an egg. But you have today and tomorrow ahead, and God still has work for you to do.

The Bible is filled with stories of people who failed yet were recommissioned by God. Jonah failed and was recommissioned. Peter failed and was recommissioned. Maybe you have failed—but God can recommission you as well. I once again refer you to the wonderful promise of Jeremiah 29:11 in which God tells us, "I know the thoughts that I think toward you, says the Lord, thoughts of peace and not of evil, to give you a future and a hope."

God has a future and a hope for you. He knows what you are going through right now. But He is telling you to be courageous because He is with you and He will give you future opportunities to serve Him despite your mistakes. As the Scripture promises us, "He who has begun a good work in you will complete it until the day of Jesus Christ" (Philippians 1:6).

Maybe you have made some mistakes and become side-tracked in your service to the Lord. Perhaps you have failed to be a spiritual leader in your home or been neglectful about sharing your faith. Maybe you have put off studying your Bible as you should or squandered the resources God has given you instead of investing them in the kingdom of God.

Be encouraged! God is giving you a hope and a future. You can't change the past, but you can start today on what God has yet for you to do. Don't sit back and say, "Because of my past, there is no future for me." There is. Leave the past behind and make a change. Learn from your mistakes and recognize your failures, but stay on course and finish the race with joy.

Take courage, because the Lord is with you and knows what you are going through. He has promised to stand by you and He has special opportunities awaiting you. Take hold of those future opportunities with both hands, realizing that His power, His presence, and His promises will give you courage.

CHAPTER FOURTEEN

$\mathcal{W}$EATHERING
LIFE'S STORMS

IN THE LAST CHAPTER WE LEFT Paul in a lonely Jerusalem prison cell. During the early hours of his imprisonment he was discouraged and fearful, wondering if his life and ministry were over. But Jesus appeared to him during those difficult moments and said, "Be of good cheer, Paul; for as you have testified for Me in Jerusalem, so you must also bear witness at Rome" (Acts 23:11). Having received new marching orders from the Lord Himself, Paul took courage. Little did he know what storms lay ahead as he followed the Lord's direction.

Paul realized he would not receive justice in the kangaroo court presided over by the Roman official, Festus, and the Jewish king, Herod Agrippa II, so the apostle exercised his right as a Roman citizen and appealed to Caesar. He probably reasoned that this strategy was his fastest track to Rome, where Jesus said he would bear witness. Sure enough, Paul's appeal worked. Festus had no choice but to send him to Rome. So Paul was put on a ship headed to Rome in the care of a Roman centurion and a group of soldiers. Acts 27 and 28 record the journey.

Even though Paul had been encouraged and redirected by the Lord Himself and was on his way to do the will of God, he still had some tough times. Sometimes we think that following the will of God means all green lights and smooth sailing. But often it's just the opposite. Doors shut in our face, obstacles block our path, and storms threaten to knock us off course. During these times of testing it is important to remember that there is a devil who wants to stop us from doing what God has asked us to do. If you are seeking to obey the Lord, expect opposition. Expect obstacles. Expect difficulties. But also expect that God will see you through.

Because Paul had a passion for God and was committed to spreading the gospel, no obstacle was big enough to stop him. He always seemed to rise above his circumstances. As he weathered the storms—both literal and figurative—on his journey to Rome, he drew strength from knowing he was obeying God. He would let nothing deter him from that course.

Captivated by Crisis

When the ship encountered rough weather on the early leg of the journey, Paul advised the crew to wait it out at a safe port. But his warning went unheeded. These seasoned sailors probably thought, *What does this landlubber know about sailing?* Soon they found themselves in a terrible storm and despaired for their lives. Suddenly Paul's earlier warning took on a ring of credibility.

In much the same way, we Christians are aware of many things which escape the notice of unbelievers. Some people believe that the growing problems of our planet can be solved by the efforts of man enabling all nations to live in peace and harmony. But any student of Scripture knows that this will never happen. We know that politicians cannot solve our problems. We know that environmentalists cannot solve our problems. We know that the nations will not be able to resolve all their differences and live in harmony. In fact, we even know from the Bible that it will get worse before it gets better!

We know mankind cannot create utopia on earth. We know that judgment will ultimately come. Like Paul, we warn people about it and call them to put their trust in Christ; but they often laugh at us and dismiss our words.

When a crisis hits, however, they begin listening with great interest. I find it interesting that many in the general public scoff at the Christian belief that the final battle, the battle of Armageddon, will be fought in the Middle East. Yet any outbreak of war in this region causes a resurgence of church attendance. The pews in our church were packed during the Persian Gulf war. People were listening with new ears because they thought, *This might be the end and I want to be ready to meet the Lord.*

I never taught that Operation Desert Storm was Armageddon because I didn't believe the Scriptures indicated it was. Still, I received numerous calls from television stations and newspapers asking for my perspective on the Gulf War and Armageddon. When the war ended, most of the new people who flocked to church as the bombs started dropping disappeared. They will be back when the next crisis hits. That's how some people are.

Peace in the Midst of the Storm

As the storm pounded the ship and threatened to break it apart and drown them all, Paul offered an unusual piece of advice to the frightened crew and passengers: "Take heart, men" (Acts 27:25). I'm sure the others probably thought, *How can we take heart? The ship is ready to fall apart and we're all going to die!* But Paul's confidence and hope were built on what he knew about God, which far outweighed what he feared about the storm.

Many times when tragedy, crisis, or hard times strike, we ask God for an immediate airlift out of the situation. Often, however, God's will for us is to learn through the very storm we are trying to escape. Romans 8:35,37 says, "Who shall separate us from the love of Christ? Shall tribulation, or distress, or persecution, or famine, or nakedness, or peril, or sword? . . . In all these things we are more than conquerors through Him who loved us." Notice that the passage says "*in* all these things." It doesn't say that God will necessarily take us *out* of tribulation, distress, etc. But it says we are more than conquerors *in* them.

How did Paul find this peace in the midst of his life-threatening storm? How can we find peace in the storms that threaten to swamp our lives and extinguish our fire for God? Allow me to present four principles from Paul's experience that will help us burn brightly in the midst of our storms.

1. God is with us in the storm. Paul could say, "Take heart, men," in the raging storm because "there stood by me this night an angel of the God to whom I belong and whom I serve, saying, 'Do not be afraid'" (Acts 27:23,24). God stood by Paul's side in the storm. In the same way, God is beside you in your storms. You may not see an angel or hear God's audible voice, but if you pay attention you will hear the still, small voice of God. Certainly He will speak to you through His Word. Then you, like Paul, can reassure others that the Lord is in control.

Time and again God reminded Paul of His presence, no doubt when he needed it most. He knew when Paul could use extra assurance. The Lord appeared to him in that prison cell in Jerusalem and told him to be courageous. Later, while being held alone in the Mamertine prison in Rome, Paul penned these words: "At my first defense no one stood with me. . . . But the Lord stood with me and strengthened me" (2 Timothy 4:16,17).

You can take heart in the face of danger or uncertainty because of your awareness of God's presence. When your employer says, "I'm sorry, but I'm going to have to let you go"; when the telephone rings and someone says, "There's been an accident"; when the doctor tells you, "I have some bad news"; when your heart sinks and you feel like your life is going to fall apart, remember: The Lord is with you. You are not alone. He is standing there by your side.

No, there are not always easy answers. Nor will you be able to explain logically why bad things happen. But you can be sure of this: He is with you through the storm. He will stand by your side just as He stood by Paul.

2. We belong to God. The second great truth that brings us peace in the midst of a storm is that we belong to God. Paul told his fellow travelers that he had been comforted by the God "to whom I belong." Do you belong to God? If so you can take heart, because God takes good care of His possessions.

There are many ways in Scripture by which God reminds us that we belong to Him. We are called His *bride.* In the Song of Solomon we read, "My beloved is mine, and I am his" (2:16). Here Solomon is speaking of the romance and love between a man and a woman, but he is also describing our relationship to God. The analogy of marriage is used throughout Scripture to describe the bond between God and His people. Christ is described as the husband of the church, His bride. In essence, we are married to God, which brings special intimacy and closeness to our relationship.

We are called His *sheep*. It's interesting that the Bible compares us to sheep instead of other animals. Dogs are relatively intelligent, so why didn't He liken us to them? Or He could have said, "My dolphins hear My voice." That would have been a more flattering comparison. Sheep are known for their stupidity, for going astray and following others even if it leads to their own destruction. They are known for making the same mistakes over and over again and for being easy prey for predators.

Unfortunately, the comparison fits. We need to belong to someone who will care for us in our weakness and vulnerability to predators. Thank God that we have a Shepherd who looks out for us!

The Bible also refers to us as God's *children*. First John 3:1 says, "Behold what manner of love the Father has bestowed on us, that we should be called the children of God!" Romans 8:15 says, "For you did not receive the spirit of bondage again to fear, but you received the Spirit of adoption by whom we cry out, 'Abba, Father.'" These verses remind us of God's fatherly tenderness and protection over each one of us.

The Bible also tells us that we are His *property*. First Corinthians 6:19,20 says, "Do you not know that your body is the temple of the Holy Spirit . . . and you are not your own? For you were bought at a price." We are the property of God Himself, who paid for us with the blood of His Son.

An elderly gentleman once was asked by a friend what he did when he was tempted. The old man replied, "Well, I just look up to heaven and say, 'Lord, Your property is in danger.'" I like that. We are God's private property, and nothing happens to us without His consent.

You can be at peace in the storm because you belong to God. He loves you as a husband loves his wife. He protects you as a shepherd protects his sheep. He tenderly cares for you as a father cares for his child. And He watches over you because you are His personal property.

3. We are about God's business. Third, Paul's heart burned brightly in the midst of the storm because he knew he was about God's business. Paul was a man under orders to the God "whom I serve." He was going where God had instructed him to go and he knew God would take care of him on the trip.

If you are injured on the job, most companies today insure you, and your medical costs are largely or completely paid. When you're on company time doing company work, the company takes care of you. Similarly, we as obedient Christians are under the Lord's protection. When we are doing His work and His will, we are under His protection and He is going to take care of us. When we stray away from what He has called us to do, however, we should not expect His blessing and protection. In fact, it might be the lack of His blessing and protection that brings us to our senses and causes us to return to Him.

4. God is faithful. Paul was comforted in the midst of the storm because of his confidence in the faithfulness of God. We see Paul's confidence in Acts 27:25 when he says, "Take heart, men, for I believe God that it will be just as it was told me." Loose paraphrase: "The Lord has always seen me through, and He's going to finish what He has begun on this trip."

Paul always seems to rise to the top of every situation, seizing every opportunity to preach the gospel. We saw him do it with Silas by sharing the gospel with the very jailer who chained them up in the dungeon. Then we saw him turn the tables for the gospel before the leaders and dignitaries of Rome. He didn't seem to be afraid of anything.

Now here he is, a passenger giving orders to the crew, the soldiers, the captain, and the Roman centurion. He starts out as a prisoner and ends up drafting the battle plan for surviving the storm and giving a pep talk to his terrified fellow travelers. No, his life wasn't always easy. In fact, it was often tremendously difficult. But the words he wrote in Philippians tell his secret: "I have learned in whatever state I am, to be content" (4:11). He was fully convinced of God's faithfulness to work through him in all situations.

God's Will and Man's Choice

Paul's experience in the storm at sea provides us with a wonderful illustration of two truths which are often thought to be in conflict: the sovereignty and preordained will of God and the free will of man. At the height of the storm, as some of the sailors on board were attempting to jump ship, Paul warned the centurion and the soldiers in Acts 27:31, "Unless these men stay in the ship, you cannot be saved."

Do you see the significance of this statement to our story? On one hand, the angel assured Paul in verse 24 that every man in the boat would survive. Only the boat would be lost. Now Paul indicates that some could die if they didn't stay with the ship. Is this a contradiction? Didn't God say that Paul and all who traveled with him would reach their destination safely? Yes, but there was one condition that must be met: staying aboard ship.

The captain might have said, "What difference does it make, Paul? You told us that we're all going to be safe anyway. It doesn't make any difference what anybody does. If God has foreordained it, it will happen." And Paul would have responded, "Yes, it makes a great deal of difference what individuals do. Yes, you will all be saved—but you must stay on the ship to take advantage of God's protection."

This story clearly shows how God's will and man's response work hand in hand. The church has debated the issue of the sovereignty of God and the free will of man for centuries. On one side of this argument we have those who believe that God will accomplish His plan with or without the cooperation of man. On the other side we have those who place overwhelming emphasis on man's response to God's will.

Some say these truths are not compatible because they cancel each other out. In other words, if you believe that God has preordained everything and He is in control, you cannot believe man has any freedom of choice. You must either be a proponent of God's sovereignty or man's choice, they say. You can't have both.

I'm sorry, but I can't choose between them. As far as I can see, both are clearly taught in Scripture, as this story illustrates. Therefore, I believe both. I don't believe they cancel each other out. Harry Ironside once said, "Human responsibility is just one spoke in the great wheel of God's purpose, and divine foreordination is another."

Some take the concept of predestination out of context, like the sailors who were trying to escape. These are the people who say, "Well, I'm saved and I know that I've been predestined, so I can go out and live as I want. I can break the commandments of God and sin up a storm because I'm already in the fold."

No, you must "stay on the ship," so to speak. You must seek to stay close to Jesus Christ and abide in Him. God has done His part to save you; you must do your part by living responsibly within His will and His Word.

Homeward Bound

Paul did indeed make it to Rome on this trip and had a fruitful ministry for two years. He later returned to Rome for one final visit. But his experience this time was not pleasant. The Mamertine Prison was nothing more than a cold, dark cave. No sanitation facilities. No windows. No ventilation. Food was lowered to the prisoners through a hole in the top.

It was in this cave that Paul wrote his final letter, the book of Second Timothy. He could have been depressed. He could have been despondent. He could have been disappointed and said, "God, why did You allow this to happen to me?" But Paul's life ended on a note of victory, not defeat: "I have fought the good fight, I have finished the race, I have kept the faith. Finally, there is laid up for me the crown of righteousness, which the Lord, the righteous Judge, will give to me on that Day, and not to me only but also to all who have loved His appearing" (2 Timothy 4:7,8).

We do not have a record of Paul's meeting with the emperor of Rome, although church tradition tells us that he finally confronted Nero. It is worth noting that it was not long after Paul's imprisonment that Nero began his relentless persecution of Christians, a fact which is historically documented. This wicked leader was responsible for torturing and executing many followers of Jesus Christ.

Nero was demented and possibly demon-possessed. He held contests in the arenas in which Christians were fed to the lions. Believers could only be spared if they renounced their faith. Others were tortured and pulled apart on racks. Nero even covered some unrecanting believers with pitch and lit them on fire, using them as human torches in his garden while he rode through in his chariot, naked and laughing.

Some have wondered if this horrendous behavior began after he met the apostle Paul. Although we cannot prove it, it's possible that Paul appeared before Nero and, as he had with the other Roman rulers, presented the gospel, laying it on the line. In fact, Paul probably gave Nero both barrels, thinking, *This is my one shot. This is going to count. Maybe this man will come to faith.*

If that was the case, Nero's violent reaction typifies the response of unbelievers who utterly harden their hearts and reject the gospel. Ironically, often those who are the most vocal in opposing the gospel are the ones who are under the greatest conviction of the Spirit.

Finally, Paul's life on earth ended. Again, we have no record of how Paul died, but church tradition tells us he was beheaded. Contrast his glorious statement of victory in 2 Timothy 4:7,8 with the sad words of King Solomon, who was known for his fabulous wisdom and wealth. He lived a much more comfortable life than Paul, yet turned out to be a fool. Looking back over his life, Solomon said, "I looked on all the works that my hands had done and on the labor in which I had toiled; and indeed all was vanity and grasping for the wind. There was no profit under the sun" (Ecclesiastes 2:11).

What a tragedy to look back over your life and say such a thing. How much better to say with Paul, "I fought the good fight. I finished the race. I kept the faith."

No wonder Paul turned his world rightside up! He learned how to weather the many violent storms in his life and keep the passion of his love for Christ burning steadily. Perhaps none of us will come close to suffering for Christ as this great apostle did. But no matter. As we learn to recognize God's presence and power as Paul did in whatever storms we face, we will enjoy the same victory at life's end.

CHAPTER FIFTEEN

LIVING OUT YOUR PRIORITIES

NOT MANY PEOPLE HAVE read their own obituary. Alfred Nobel did. Nobel had been ill and someone falsely reported that he died. Imagine his surprise when he opened the newspaper one morning and saw his own death notice!

As he read through the brief paragraphs that summarized his life and work, he became disturbed to find that he was noted only as the man who invented dynamite. The obituary further described all the destruction his invention had caused. Nobel deplored the thought of being remembered as the creator of something that had been used to destroy so many lives.

After reading his obituary, Nobel decided to make a change. He dedicated his life to a new direction: the pursuit of peace. And today we remember Alfred Nobel not as the inventor of dynamite, but as the founder of the Nobel Peace Prize.

Nobel's story illustrates an important truth: It is never too late to change the direction of your life.

What if you knew that today was your last day on earth? How would you sum up your life and ministry? What truths would you emphasize to your friends and family? What have you learned about God and His Word over the years? Would you be able to say with the apostle Paul that you finished your race with joy—or would you look back on life with regret?

I heard Dr. Alan Redpath speak some years ago. He was a great Bible teacher and a wonderful man of God who has now gone on to be with his Lord. He told how, as a young English Christian, he heard a statement in a sermon that turned his life around: "You can have a saved soul and a lost life." Dr. Redpath couldn't get those words out of his mind. His soul was saved, but his life was going nowhere. From that moment on he committed himself to follow the Lord so that his life would count for something.

Have you made the same discovery? Are you aware that there is more to having a passion for God than just making sure you're on your way to heaven? For the early Christians, being heaven-bound and Spirit-filled wasn't an end in itself. They wanted their everyday lives to count for eternity. They were zealous for God and they were committed to turning their world rightside up in the power of the risen Christ they so faithfully served.

Have you made that same commitment, or will your obituary reflect a saved soul and a lost life? Until you give yourself wholeheartedly to living out the priorities the early believers followed, you will fail to realize your potential in the power of the Spirit for touching the world around you.

The Responsible Watchman

Toward the close of his ministry, the apostle Paul made a statement that helps us understand what it means to be a passionate believer in a world of needy people. He was addressing the elders in the church at Ephesus on the eve of his departure for Rome. The statement he made in Acts 20:26 is—next to 2 Timothy 4:6-8—perhaps the most dramatic and sobering description of his life and ministry: "I am innocent of the blood of all men" (Acts 20:26).

Paul's words relate to the Lord's statement to Ezekiel in Ezekiel 3:17-19: "Son of man, I have made you a watchman for the house of Israel; therefore hear a word from My mouth, and give them warning from Me: when I say to the wicked, 'You shall surely die,' and you give him no warning, nor speak to warn the wicked from his wicked way, to save his life, that same wicked man shall die in his iniquity; but his blood I will require at your hand. Yet, if you warn the wicked, and he does not turn from his wickedness, nor from his wicked way, he shall die in his iniquity; but you have delivered your soul."

In Ezekiel's day, watchmen sat on the walls of the city scanning the countryside for danger. They were to stay awake and alert, ready to sound the alarm if they spied enemy forces or any other kind of approaching danger. Because the safety of many was at stake, the city held the watchmen responsible if they failed to warn the people of danger.

Paul knew that if he failed to preach the message of the gospel, the blood of many would be on his hands. He informed the Ephesian elders that he had done what was required of him. He had preached the gospel faithfully to everyone God had brought into his life. He was free from the blood of all men.

Likewise, we have been given a message and God calls us to be vigilant and responsible to proclaim it. Pay careful attention here. God has not called us to convert people; I can't convert anyone, nor can you. He *has* called us to proclaim His message. Conversion is the work of the Holy Spirit alone. Our responsibility is to declare the truth about Jesus Christ. Once we've declared the truth to someone, we are no longer responsible for his or her blood. If we tell them the good news and they reject it, there's nothing we can do about it. We've done our part. We've fulfilled our responsibility. We may continue to pray and share with that person, but if they refuse to come to faith, God will not hold us responsible.

Paul went on to tell the Ephesians, "I have not shunned to declare to you the whole counsel of God" (Acts 20:27). The word Paul used for "shunned" is a nautical term meaning to take in the sail. Some of us are willing to talk about God when the circumstances are right, but if there is any likelihood of embarrassment or ridicule, we pull in the sail and keep our mouths shut. We shun declaring everything God wants us to declare.

Paul said, "I never pulled in the sail. I declared the truth, the whole truth, and nothing but the truth. My hands are clean." Can you say that about yourself and your witness for Christ? If you died today, and those who knew you wrote your obituary, would they confidently state that you lived "full sail" for Christ and took full advantage of every opportunity to share the gospel?

A Life Worth Remembering

I've done quite a few memorial services as a pastor. It's sad when there isn't much to say about a person's life. In services like these, eulogies about how wonderful, kind, and selfless the person was make you wonder if it's the same person you knew!

On the other hand, what a joy it is to attend a memorial service for someone who lived out Christ's priorities as his own. We say with confidence, "This person was in love with Jesus Christ and always had time for others. This person was a faithful watchman. All who knew him had an opportunity to hear the gospel."

What will be spoken at your memorial service? What will be written in your obituary? Alfred Nobel read his own obituary and made some changes. You can make some changes right now. Maybe you need to get back on course by living out Christ's priorities in your life. Or perhaps you need to get on course for the first time because you recognize that, although your soul is saved, your life hasn't counted for eternity.

A good place to start is to respond positively to God's call and start using the gifts He has given you for His kingdom. As the saying goes, "Only one life, 'twill soon be past; only what's done for Christ will last." Everything else in life will pass away. All else will be forgotten. Only what you do for the Lord and for His kingdom will be remembered.

D.L. Moody was challenged as a young man by a wise old Christian gentleman who said, "You know, Moody, the world has yet to see what God will do with and for and through and in and by the man who is fully and wholly consecrated to Him." Moody's response was, "I will try my utmost to be that man." He sure came close. He went on to become the Billy Graham of his generation.

I wonder if you can say, "I want to be that person who is totally committed to God. I want to have a passion for Him and see what He can do in and through me." If you can say that, your life will make a difference as God's power enables you to be a responsible watchman for Him.

God wants to do many things in your world, but the Scripture reminds us that He seeks faithful servants through whom to work: "The eyes of the Lord run to and fro throughout the whole earth, to show Himself strong on behalf of those whose heart is loyal to Him" (2 Chronicles 16:9). Will you step forward and say, "Here I am, Lord. Send me. Show Yourself strong on my behalf. I'm available"?

If you do, you'll be amazed to see what God will do through you in the days ahead. I challenge you to revive your passion for Him by living out this commitment day by day. Your world will never be the same.

Other Good
Harvest House Reading

GOD'S DESIGN FOR CHRISTIAN DATING
by *Greg Laurie*

In the midst of conflicting worldly standards, it is still possible to find and fulfill God's design for exciting relationships with the opposite sex. This book offers godly counsel with touches of humor on healthy dating.

EVERY DAY WITH JESUS
by *Greg Laurie*

Evangelist and pastor of one of America's largest churches, Greg Laurie explores having an intimate relationship with Jesus in devotions based on Luke. Readers are encouraged and given resources to tackle today's difficult situations.

DISCIPLESHIP
by *Greg Laurie*

Every disciple is a believer but not every believer is a disciple. Popular pastor and evangelist Greg Laurie takes readers to the roots of dynamic faith and provides the nourishment they need to grow spiritually strong. Concise and to-the-point, every page of *Discipleship* delivers solid biblical principles and specific steps for developing the radical faith of the early church.

Dear Reader,

We would appreciate hearing from you regarding this Harvest House nonfiction book. It will enable us to continue to give you the best in Christian publishing.

1. What most influenced you to purchase *A Passion for God?*
   - ❏ Author
   - ❏ Subject matter
   - ❏ Backcover copy
   - ❏ Recommendations
   - ❏ Cover/Title
   - ❏ Other_____

2. Where did you purchase this book?
   - ❏ Christian bookstore
   - ❏ General bookstore
   - ❏ Department store
   - ❏ Grocery store
   - ❏ Other_____

3. Your overall rating of this book?
   - ❏ Excellent   ❏ Very good   ❏ Good   ❏ Fair   ❏ Poor

4. How likely would you be to purchase other books by this author?
   - ❏ Very likely   ❏ Not very likely   ❏ Somewhat likely   ❏ Not at all

5. What types of books most interest you? (Check all that apply.)
   - ❏ Women's Books
   - ❏ Marriage Books
   - ❏ Current Issues
   - ❏ Christian Living
   - ❏ Bible Studies
   - ❏ Fiction
   - ❏ Biographies
   - ❏ Children's Books
   - ❏ Youth Books
   - ❏ Other_____

6. Please check the box next to your age group.
   - ❏ Under 18   ❏ 18-24   ❏ 25-34   ❏ 35-44   ❏ 45-54   ❏ 55 and over

Mail to: Editorial Director
           Harvest House Publishers
           1075 Arrowsmith
           Eugene, OR 97402

Name _____

Address _____

State _____ Zip _____

Thank you for helping us to help you in future publications!

If you would like to know more about Greg Laurie's crusade ministry or where his radio broadcasts can be heard, you can write him at:

Harvest Crusades with Greg Laurie
6115 Arlington
Riverside, CA 92504